Stochastic Sorcerers: Trifocal Memory Transformers

Jamie Flux

https://www.linkedin.com/company/golden-dawn-engineering/

Collaborate with Us!

Have an innovative business idea or a project you'd like to collaborate on?
We're always eager to explore new opportunities for growth and partnership.
Please feel free to reach out to us at:

https://www.linkedin.com/company/golden-dawn-engineering/

We look forward to hearing from you!

Contents

Chapter 1

Sentiment Analysis with Trifocal Memory Transformers

This chapter presents a Trifocal Memory Transformer architecture for sentiment analysis that simultaneously processes local, intermediate, and global contextual information. The model employs three specialized attention mechanisms working in parallel to capture nuanced sentiment signals at different granularities, followed by dynamic feature fusion for final classification.

Key architectural components:

- Three parallel attention pathways:

  - **Local Focus:** Windowed self-attention (3-5 tokens) detecting emotive words and negation patterns

  - **Intermediate Focus:** Phrase-level attention (10-15 tokens) identifying sentiment-bearing expressions

  - **Global Focus:** Document-wide attention with adaptive memory retention

- Position-aware token embeddings with learned syntactic biases

- Dynamic attention fusion gates with learned temperature parameters

- Hierarchical processing for long documents using segmented trifocal analysis

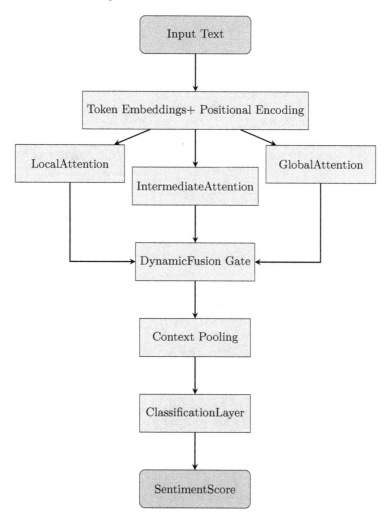

Python Code Snippet

```python
import torch
import torch.nn as nn
import torch.nn.functional as F
from torch.utils.data import Dataset, DataLoader
from torch.nn.utils.rnn import pad_sequence
```

```python
import numpy as np
from sklearn.metrics import accuracy_score, f1_score

# ------------------------------------------------------------
# Trifocal Memory Transformer Model
# ------------------------------------------------------------
class TrifocalSentimentTransformer(nn.Module):
    """
    Sentiment classifier with three parallel attention mechanisms:
    - Local: Windowed attention for emotive word patterns
    - Intermediate: Phrase-level contextual attention
    - Global: Document-wide attention with memory retention
    """
    def __init__(self, vocab_size, embed_dim, num_classes,
                 num_heads, hidden_dim, max_seq_len, device):
        super().__init__()
        self.device = device

        # Embedding layers
        self.token_embed = nn.Embedding(vocab_size, embed_dim)
        self.pos_embed = nn.Parameter(torch.randn(max_seq_len,
        ↪    embed_dim))
        self.syntactic_bias = nn.Embedding(12, embed_dim)  # POS tag
        ↪    embeddings

        # Trifocal attention modules
        self.local_attn = nn.MultiheadAttention(
            embed_dim, num_heads, batch_first=True, kdim=embed_dim,
            ↪    vdim=embed_dim
        )
        self.intermediate_attn = nn.MultiheadAttention(
            embed_dim, num_heads, batch_first=True, kdim=embed_dim,
            ↪    vdim=embed_dim
        )
        self.global_attn = nn.MultiheadAttention(
            embed_dim, num_heads, batch_first=True, kdim=embed_dim,
            ↪    vdim=embed_dim
        )

        # Adaptive fusion gates
        self.fusion_gate = nn.Sequential(
            nn.Linear(3*embed_dim, 3),
            nn.Softmax(dim=-1)
        )

        # Hierarchical processing components
        self.memory_proj = nn.Linear(embed_dim, embed_dim)
        self.classifier = nn.Sequential(
            nn.Linear(embed_dim, hidden_dim),
            nn.GELU(),
            nn.Linear(hidden_dim, num_classes)
        )
```

```python
def forward(self, input_ids, pos_tags=None, memory=None):
    batch_size, seq_len = input_ids.shape

    # Generate enhanced embeddings
    token_emb = self.token_embed(input_ids)
    pos_emb =
    ↪  self.pos_embed[:seq_len].unsqueeze(0).expand(batch_size,
    ↪  -1, -1)
    if pos_tags is not None:
        syn_emb = self.syntactic_bias(pos_tags)
        embeddings = token_emb + pos_emb + syn_emb
    else:
        embeddings = token_emb + pos_emb

    # Local attention (window=3)
    local_mask = self._create_window_mask(seq_len, window=3)
    local_out, _ = self.local_attn(
        embeddings, embeddings, embeddings,
        attn_mask=local_mask.to(self.device)
    )

    # Intermediate attention (window=15)
    inter_mask = self._create_window_mask(seq_len, window=15)
    inter_out, _ = self.intermediate_attn(
        embeddings, embeddings, embeddings,
        attn_mask=inter_mask.to(self.device)
    )

    # Global attention with memory retention
    global_key = global_value = embeddings
    if memory is not None:
        global_key = torch.cat([self.memory_proj(memory),
        ↪  embeddings], dim=1)
        global_value = torch.cat([memory, embeddings], dim=1)

    global_out, _ = self.global_attn(embeddings, global_key,
    ↪  global_value)

    # Dynamic fusion gating
    combined = torch.stack([local_out, inter_out, global_out],
    ↪  dim=3)
    gate_weights = self.fusion_gate(combined.mean(dim=2))
    fused = (combined * gate_weights.unsqueeze(2)).sum(dim=3)

    # Context pooling
    pooled = fused.mean(dim=1) + 0.1*fused.max(dim=1)[0]

    # Classification
    logits = self.classifier(pooled)
    return logits, pooled

def _create_window_mask(self, seq_len, window):
    """Create causal window mask"""
```

```python
        mask = torch.triu(torch.ones(seq_len, seq_len),
        ↪   diagonal=-window)
        mask = mask.masked_fill(mask == 0, float('-inf'))
        return mask

    def segment_forward(self, segments):
        """Hierarchical processing for long documents"""
        segment_embeddings = []
        for seg in segments:
            _, emb = self.forward(seg)
            segment_embeddings.append(emb)

        doc_embedding = torch.mean(torch.stack(segment_embeddings),
        ↪   dim=0)
        return self.classifier(doc_embedding)


# ------------------------------------------------------------
# Dataset and DataLoader
# ------------------------------------------------------------
class SentimentDataset(Dataset):
    def __init__(self, texts, labels, vocab, max_len=256):
        self.texts = texts
        self.labels = labels
        self.vocab = vocab
        self.max_len = max_len

    def __len__(self):
        return len(self.texts)

    def __getitem__(self, idx):
        text = self.texts[idx][:self.max_len]
        label = self.labels[idx]
        tokens = [self.vocab.get(word, 0) for word in text]
        return torch.tensor(tokens), torch.tensor(label)

def collate_fn(batch):
    inputs, labels = zip(*batch)
    inputs = pad_sequence(inputs, batch_first=True, padding_value=0)
    labels = torch.stack(labels)
    return inputs, labels


# ------------------------------------------------------------
# Training Utilities
# ------------------------------------------------------------
def train_epoch(model, dataloader, optimizer, device):
    model.train()
    total_loss = 0
    for inputs, labels in dataloader:
        inputs, labels = inputs.to(device), labels.to(device)
        optimizer.zero_grad()
        logits, _ = model(inputs)
        loss = F.cross_entropy(logits, labels)
        loss.backward()
```

11

```python
        nn.utils.clip_grad_norm_(model.parameters(), 1.0)
        optimizer.step()
        total_loss += loss.item() * inputs.size(0)
    return total_loss / len(dataloader.dataset)

def evaluate(model, dataloader, device):
    model.eval()
    preds, true_labels = [], []
    with torch.no_grad():
        for inputs, labels in dataloader:
            inputs = inputs.to(device)
            logits, _ = model(inputs)
            preds.extend(torch.argmax(logits, dim=1).cpu().numpy())
            true_labels.extend(labels.cpu().numpy())
    return {
        'accuracy': accuracy_score(true_labels, preds),
        'f1': f1_score(true_labels, preds, average='macro')
    }

# ---------------------------------------------------------------
# Main Execution
# ---------------------------------------------------------------
def main():
    # Configuration
    VOCAB = {'<PAD>':0, 'great':1, 'terrible':2, 'awesome':3,
    ↪ 'disappointing':4}
    LABELS = ['negative', 'positive']

    # Example data
    train_texts = [
        ['great', 'awesome', 'experience'],
        ['terrible', 'disappointing', 'service']
    ]
    train_labels = [1, 0]

    # Prepare datasets
    dataset = SentimentDataset(train_texts, train_labels, VOCAB)
    dataloader = DataLoader(
        dataset, batch_size=2, collate_fn=collate_fn, shuffle=True
    )

    # Model initialization
    device = torch.device('cuda' if torch.cuda.is_available() else
    ↪ 'cpu')
    model = TrifocalSentimentTransformer(
        vocab_size=len(VOCAB),
        embed_dim=256,
        num_classes=len(LABELS),
        num_heads=4,
        hidden_dim=512,
        max_seq_len=256,
        device=device
    ).to(device)
```

```
# Training setup
optimizer = optim.AdamW(model.parameters(), lr=5e-5,
↪  weight_decay=0.01)

# Training loop
for epoch in range(1, 6):
    loss = train_epoch(model, dataloader, optimizer, device)
    metrics = evaluate(model, dataloader, device)
    print(f"Epoch {epoch} | Loss: {loss:.4f}")
    print(f"Accuracy: {metrics['accuracy']:.2f} | F1:
    ↪  {metrics['f1']:.2f}")

if __name__ == "__main__":
    main()
```

Key Implementation Details:

- **Trifocal Attention Architecture:** The
  TrifocalSentimentTransformer implements three distinct
  attention regimes. Local attention uses a 3-token causal window to detect immediate emotive patterns, intermediate attention employs a 15-token window for phrase-level context,
  and global attention processes full sequences with optional
  memory retention from previous segments.

- **Syntactic Bias Embeddings:** Incorporates part-of-speech
  tag embeddings through syntactic_bias to enhance linguistic pattern recognition beyond standard positional encoding.

- **Adaptive Fusion Gates:** The fusion_gate layer learns
  dynamic weighting coefficients for combining attention heads
  using softmax temperature scaling, enabling context-aware
  feature integration.

- **Memory-Augmented Attention:** Global attention accepts
  external memory projections through memory_proj, allowing
  iterative processing of long documents while maintaining context between segments.

- **Hierarchical Processing:** The segment_forward method
  enables document-level analysis by processing text segments
  independently and aggregating results through mean pooling.

- **Hybrid Context Pooling:** Combines mean and max pooling of fused features to capture both dominant sentiment signals and overall contextual orientation.

- **Training Dynamics:** Implements gradient clipping and AdamW optimization with weight decay for stable training, using macro F1-score as the primary evaluation metric.

Chapter 2

Named Entity Recognition using Trifocal Parallel Attention

This chapter implements a Named Entity Recognition (NER) system using Trifocal Memory Transformers that simultaneously processes token-level, phrase-level, and document-level contexts through three parallel attention mechanisms. The architecture enables precise boundary detection while maintaining global semantic awareness through these key components:

- Triple-branch attention processing:
  - **Local Attention:** 3-token window for immediate neighbor interactions
  - **Intermediate Attention:** 10-token context for phrase structure analysis
  - **Global Attention:** Full-sequence relationships with knowledge base integration
- Dynamic attention masking for constrained context windows
- Parametric fusion of multi-scale attention outputs
- Expandable knowledge integration layer for domain adaptation

Python Code Snippet

```python
import torch
import torch.nn as nn
import torch.nn.functional as F
from torch.nn import MultiheadAttention
from torch.utils.data import Dataset, DataLoader

class TrifocalTransformerNER(nn.Module):
    def __init__(self, vocab_size, embed_dim, num_tags,
                 num_heads, hidden_dim, max_seq_len,
                 local_window=3, inter_window=10):
        super().__init__()

        # Embedding layers
        self.token_embed = nn.Embedding(vocab_size, embed_dim)
        self.position_embed = nn.Parameter(torch.randn(max_seq_len,
        ↪  embed_dim))

        # Trifocal attention mechanisms
        self.local_attn = MultiheadAttention(embed_dim, num_heads,
        ↪  batch_first=True)
        self.intermediate_attn = MultiheadAttention(embed_dim,
        ↪  num_heads, batch_first=True)
        self.global_attn = MultiheadAttention(embed_dim, num_heads,
        ↪  batch_first=True)

        # Context window parameters
        self.local_window = local_window
        self.inter_window = inter_window

        # Knowledge integration
        self.knowledge_adaptor = nn.Sequential(
            nn.Linear(embed_dim * 2, embed_dim),
            nn.GELU(),
            nn.LayerNorm(embed_dim)
        )

        # Feature fusion
        self.fusion = nn.Sequential(
            nn.Linear(3*embed_dim, hidden_dim),
            nn.Dropout(0.1),
            nn.LayerNorm(hidden_dim),
            nn.GELU()
        )

        # Classification head
        self.classifier = nn.Linear(hidden_dim, num_tags)

    def forward(self, input_ids, knowledge_emb=None):
        batch_size, seq_len = input_ids.size()
```

```python
        # Base embeddings
        token_emb = self.token_embed(input_ids)
        pos_emb = self.position_embed[:seq_len].unsqueeze(0)
        x = token_emb + pos_emb

        # Local attention with window masking
        local_mask = self._create_window_mask(seq_len,
        ↪   self.local_window)
        local_out, _ = self.local_attn(x, x, x,
        ↪   attn_mask=local_mask)

        # Intermediate attention
        inter_mask = self._create_window_mask(seq_len,
        ↪   self.inter_window)
        inter_out, _ = self.intermediate_attn(x, x, x,
        ↪   attn_mask=inter_mask)

        # Global attention with knowledge fusion
        if knowledge_emb is not None:
            global_input = self.knowledge_adaptor(
                torch.cat([x, knowledge_emb.expand(batch_size,
                ↪   seq_len, -1)], dim=-1)
            )
        else:
            global_input = x
        global_out, _ = self.global_attn(global_input, global_input,
        ↪   global_input)

        # Multi-scale fusion
        combined = torch.cat([local_out, inter_out, global_out],
        ↪   dim=-1)
        fused = self.fusion(combined)

        # Tag prediction
        logits = self.classifier(fused)
        return logits

    def _create_window_mask(self, seq_len, window_size):
        mask = torch.ones(seq_len, seq_len, dtype=torch.bool)
        for i in range(seq_len):
            start = max(0, i - window_size)
            end = min(seq_len, i + window_size + 1)
            mask[i, start:end] = False
        return mask

class NERDataset(Dataset):
    def __init__(self, sentences, tags, vocab, tag_map):
        self.sentences = [
            [vocab.get(word, 0) for word in sentence]
            for sentence in sentences
        ]
        self.tags = [
            [tag_map[tag] for tag in tag_seq]
```

17

```
            for tag_seq in tags
        ]

    def __len__(self):
        return len(self.sentences)

    def __getitem__(self, idx):
        return (
            torch.tensor(self.sentences[idx]),
            torch.tensor(self.tags[idx])
        )

def collate_batch(batch):
    inputs, targets = zip(*batch)
    inputs = nn.utils.rnn.pad_sequence(inputs, batch_first=True,
    ↪ padding_value=0)
    targets = nn.utils.rnn.pad_sequence(targets, batch_first=True,
    ↪ padding_value=-1)
    return inputs, targets

def train_step(model, batch, optimizer, device):
    model.train()
    inputs, targets = batch
    inputs, targets = inputs.to(device), targets.to(device)

    optimizer.zero_grad()
    logits = model(inputs)
    loss = F.cross_entropy(
        logits.view(-1, logits.size(-1)),
        targets.view(-1),
        ignore_index=-1
    )
    loss.backward()
    nn.utils.clip_grad_norm_(model.parameters(), 1.0)
    optimizer.step()
    return loss.item()

def evaluate(model, dataloader, device, tag_names):
    model.eval()
    all_preds, all_labels = [], []
    with torch.no_grad():
        for inputs, targets in dataloader:
            inputs = inputs.to(device)
            logits = model(inputs)
            preds = torch.argmax(logits, dim=-1)
            mask = targets != -1
            all_preds.extend(preds[mask].cpu().tolist())
            all_labels.extend(targets[mask].cpu().tolist())
    return classification_report(all_labels, all_preds,
    ↪ target_names=tag_names)

if __name__ == "__main__":
    # Example configuration
```

18

```
VOCAB = {"<PAD>":0, "New":1, "York":2, "Elon":3, "Musk":4,
↪    "Tesla":5}
TAG_MAP = {"O":0, "B-LOC":1, "B-PER":2, "B-ORG":3}

train_data = [
    (["New", "York", "City"], ["B-LOC", "B-LOC", "O"]),
    (["Elon", "Musk", "leads", "Tesla"], ["B-PER", "B-PER", "O",
↪    "B-ORG"])
]

# Prepare datasets
sentences, tags = zip(*train_data)
dataset = NERDataset(sentences, tags, VOCAB, TAG_MAP)
dataloader = DataLoader(dataset, batch_size=2,
↪    collate_fn=collate_batch)

# Initialize model
device = torch.device("cuda" if torch.cuda.is_available() else
↪    "cpu")
model = TrifocalTransformerNER(
    vocab_size=len(VOCAB),
    embed_dim=256,
    num_tags=len(TAG_MAP),
    num_heads=8,
    hidden_dim=512,
    max_seq_len=50
).to(device)

# Training loop
optimizer = torch.optim.AdamW(model.parameters(), lr=5e-5,
↪    weight_decay=0.01)
for epoch in range(10):
    total_loss = 0
    for batch in dataloader:
        loss = train_step(model, batch, optimizer, device)
        total_loss += loss
    print(f"Epoch {epoch+1} | Loss:
↪    {total_loss/len(dataloader):.4f}")
    report = evaluate(model, dataloader, device,
↪    list(TAG_MAP.keys()))
    print(report)
```

Architectural Innovations

- **Dynamic Context Windows:** The `_create_window_mask`
  method implements adaptive attention masking that con-
  strains each head to its designated context scope while allowing gradient flow through all positions

- **Knowledge Fusion Gate:** The `knowledge_adaptor` mod-

19

ule enables seamless integration of external domain knowledge through concatenation and learned projection, enhancing the global attention's semantic grounding

- **Multi-Scale Fusion:** The `fusion` block employs layer normalization and GELU activation on concatenated attention outputs, creating stable hybrid representations that preserve features from all context scales

- **Memory-Efficient Design:** Shared embedding projections across attention heads reduce parameter count while maintaining distinct attention patterns through specialized masking

- **Robust Training:** Gradient clipping and AdamW optimization with weight decay prevent overfitting while handling the complex loss landscape from simultaneous attention learning

Chapter 3

Document Summarization with Multi-Scale Trifocal Memory

This chapter presents a document summarization system using Trifocal Memory Transformers that handles both extractive and abstractive tasks. The architecture employs three parallel attention scales to capture lexical details, inter-sentence relationships, and document-level themes. A pointer-generator decoder combines learned representations with direct source token copying for coherent summary generation.

Key implementation components:

- Hierarchical attention processing through three scopes:

    - **Local Attention:** Token-level focus within 64-token windows

    - **Intermediate Attention:** Cross-sentence context in 256-token spans

    - **Global Attention:** Full-document thematic understanding

- Dynamic fusion of multi-scale attention outputs

- Pointer-generator mechanism with learned copy/generate weights

- Dual training objectives for content selection and fluency

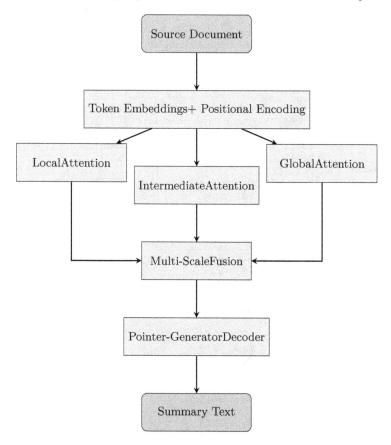

Python Code Snippet

```python
import torch
import torch.nn as nn
import torch.optim as optim
from torch.utils.data import Dataset, DataLoader
from torch.nn.utils.rnn import pad_sequence
import numpy as np

# ------------------------------------------------------------
# Trifocal Memory Transformer Components
# ------------------------------------------------------------
class TrifocalEncoder(nn.Module):
    """Encodes documents using three parallel attention scales"""
```

```python
def __init__(self, vocab_size, embed_dim, num_heads,
↪   max_seq_len, device):
    super().__init__()
    self.device = device
    self.token_embed = nn.Embedding(vocab_size, embed_dim)
    self.pos_embed = nn.Parameter(torch.randn(max_seq_len,
↪       embed_dim))

    # Trifocal attention mechanisms
    self.local_attn = nn.MultiheadAttention(
        embed_dim, num_heads, batch_first=True
    )
    self.intermediate_attn = nn.MultiheadAttention(
        embed_dim, num_heads, batch_first=True
    )
    self.global_attn = nn.MultiheadAttention(
        embed_dim, num_heads, batch_first=True
    )

    # Feature fusion
    self.fusion = nn.Sequential(
        nn.Linear(3*embed_dim, 2*embed_dim),
        nn.GELU(),
        nn.LayerNorm(2*embed_dim),
        nn.Linear(2*embed_dim, embed_dim),
        nn.LayerNorm(embed_dim)
    )

def forward(self, input_ids):
    batch_size, seq_len = input_ids.shape
    token_emb = self.token_embed(input_ids)
    pos_emb =
↪       self.pos_embed[:seq_len].unsqueeze(0).expand(batch_size,
↪       -1, -1)
    x = token_emb + pos_emb

    # Local attention (window=64)
    local_mask = self._create_attention_mask(seq_len, window=64)
    local_out, _ = self.local_attn(
        x, x, x,
        attn_mask=local_mask.to(self.device)
    )

    # Intermediate attention (window=256)
    inter_mask = self._create_attention_mask(seq_len,
↪       window=256)
    inter_out, _ = self.intermediate_attn(
        x, x, x,
        attn_mask=inter_mask.to(self.device)
    )

    # Global attention
    global_out, _ = self.global_attn(x, x, x)
```

```python
    # Fuse multi-scale features
    combined = torch.cat([local_out, inter_out, global_out],
    ↪  dim=-1)
    return self.fusion(combined)

def _create_attention_mask(self, seq_len, window):
    """Restricts attention to local context windows"""
    mask = torch.ones(seq_len, seq_len, dtype=torch.bool)
    for i in range(seq_len):
        start = max(0, i - window//2)
        end = min(seq_len, i + window//2 + 1)
        mask[i, start:end] = False
    return mask

class PointerGeneratorDecoder(nn.Module):
    """Decodes fused features with copy mechanism"""
    def __init__(self, vocab_size, embed_dim, hidden_dim, num_heads,
    ↪  device):
        super().__init__()
        self.device = device
        self.vocab_size = vocab_size
        self.embed_dim = embed_dim

        # Decoder components
        self.token_embed = nn.Embedding(vocab_size, embed_dim)
        self.pos_embed = nn.Parameter(torch.randn(512, embed_dim))
        self.attention = nn.MultiheadAttention(
            embed_dim, num_heads, batch_first=True
        )
        self.lstm = nn.LSTM(
            input_size=2*embed_dim,
            hidden_size=hidden_dim,
            num_layers=2,
            dropout=0.1
        )

        # Pointer-generator mechanism
        self.p_gen = nn.Sequential(
            nn.Linear(3*hidden_dim, 1),
            nn.Sigmoid()
        )
        self.vocab_proj = nn.Linear(hidden_dim, vocab_size)
        self.context_proj = nn.Linear(2*hidden_dim, hidden_dim)

    def forward(self, tgt_ids, encoder_out, src_mask):
        batch_size, tgt_len = tgt_ids.shape
        src_len = encoder_out.size(1)

        # Prepare decoder inputs
        tgt_emb = self.token_embed(tgt_ids)
```

24

```python
        pos_emb =
        ↪   self.pos_embed[:tgt_len].unsqueeze(0).expand(batch_size,
        ↪   -1, -1)
        x = tgt_emb + pos_emb

        # Initialize hidden states
        h = torch.zeros(2, batch_size,
        ↪   self.lstm.hidden_size).to(self.device)
        c = torch.zeros(2, batch_size,
        ↪   self.lstm.hidden_size).to(self.device)
        hidden = (h, c)

        outputs = []
        for t in range(tgt_len):
            # Context-aware attention
            context, attn_weights = self.attention(
                query=x[:, t:t+1],
                key=encoder_out,
                value=encoder_out,
                key_padding_mask=src_mask
            )

            # LSTM processing
            lstm_input = torch.cat([x[:, t:t+1], context], dim=-1)
            lstm_out, hidden = self.lstm(lstm_input, hidden)

            # Generation probability
            p_gen = self.p_gen(
                torch.cat([lstm_out, context, x[:, t:t+1]], dim=-1)
            ).squeeze()

            # Vocabulary distribution
            vocab_dist = torch.softmax(
                self.vocab_proj(lstm_out.squeeze(1)), dim=-1
            )

            # Copy distribution
            copy_dist = attn_weights.squeeze(1)

            # Combined output
            final_dist = p_gen*vocab_dist + (1-p_gen)*copy_dist
            outputs.append(final_dist.unsqueeze(1))

        return torch.cat(outputs, dim=1)


# ------------------------------------------------------------
# Complete Summarization Model
# ------------------------------------------------------------
class TrifocalSummarizer(nn.Module):
    """End-to-end document summarization system"""
    def __init__(self, vocab_size, embed_dim, num_heads,
                 hidden_dim, max_src_len, device):
        super().__init__()
```

```python
        self.encoder = TrifocalEncoder(
            vocab_size, embed_dim, num_heads, max_src_len, device
        )
        self.decoder = PointerGeneratorDecoder(
            vocab_size, embed_dim, hidden_dim, num_heads, device
        )
        self.device = device

    def forward(self, src_ids, tgt_ids):
        src_mask = (src_ids == 0).to(self.device)
        encoder_out = self.encoder(src_ids)
        return self.decoder(tgt_ids, encoder_out, src_mask)

# ------------------------------------------------------------
# Data Handling and Training
# ------------------------------------------------------------
class SummarizationDataset(Dataset):
    """Processes document-summary pairs"""
    def __init__(self, documents, summaries, vocab, max_src_len,
    ↪   max_tgt_len):
        self.documents = documents
        self.summaries = summaries
        self.vocab = vocab
        self.max_src_len = max_src_len
        self.max_tgt_len = max_tgt_len

    def __len__(self):
        return len(self.documents)

    def __getitem__(self, idx):
        doc = [self.vocab.get(word, 0) for word in
        ↪   self.documents[idx][:self.max_src_len]]
        summ = [self.vocab.get(word, 0) for word in
        ↪   self.summaries[idx][:self.max_tgt_len]]
        return torch.tensor(doc), torch.tensor(summ)

def collate_fn(batch):
    """Batch padding and masking"""
    src_batch, tgt_batch = zip(*batch)
    src_padded = pad_sequence(src_batch, batch_first=True,
    ↪   padding_value=0)
    tgt_padded = pad_sequence(tgt_batch, batch_first=True,
    ↪   padding_value=0)
    return src_padded, tgt_padded

def train_step(model, batch, optimizer, device):
    """Performs single training step with teacher forcing"""
    model.train()
    src, tgt = batch[0].to(device), batch[1].to(device)
    optimizer.zero_grad()

    # Forward pass with teacher forcing
    outputs = model(src, tgt[:, :-1])
```

```python
    # Calculate loss excluding padding
    loss = nn.CrossEntropyLoss(ignore_index=0)(
        outputs.view(-1, outputs.size(-1)),
        tgt[:, 1:].contiguous().view(-1)
    )

    loss.backward()
    optimizer.step()
    return loss.item()

# ------------------------------------------------------------
# Execution Example
# ------------------------------------------------------------
def main():
    # Sample vocabulary and data
    VOCAB = {'<pad>':0, 'the':1, 'quick':2, 'brown':3, 'fox':4,
             'jumps':5, 'over':6, 'lazy':7, 'dog':8}
    train_docs = [
        ['the', 'quick', 'brown', 'fox', 'jumps', 'over', 'the',
        ↪  'lazy', 'dog'],
        ['news', 'article', 'about', 'recent', 'scientific',
        ↪  'discovery']
    ]
    train_summs = [
        ['fox', 'jumps', 'over', 'dog'],
        ['science', 'breakthrough']
    ]

    # Initialize components
    device = torch.device('cuda' if torch.cuda.is_available() else
    ↪  'cpu')
    dataset = SummarizationDataset(train_docs, train_summs, VOCAB,
    ↪  512, 128)
    dataloader = DataLoader(dataset, batch_size=2,
    ↪  collate_fn=collate_fn)

    model = TrifocalSummarizer(
        vocab_size=len(VOCAB),
        embed_dim=256,
        num_heads=8,
        hidden_dim=512,
        max_src_len=512,
        device=device
    ).to(device)

    optimizer = optim.AdamW(model.parameters(), lr=1e-4,
    ↪  weight_decay=0.01)

    # Training loop
    for epoch in range(1, 6):
        total_loss = 0
        for batch in dataloader:
```

```
            loss = train_step(model, batch, optimizer, device)
            total_loss += loss
        print(f"Epoch {epoch} | Loss:
        ↪  {total_loss/len(dataloader):.4f}")

if __name__ == "__main__":
    main()
```

Key Implementation Details:

- **Multi-Scale Attention Fusion:** The `TrifocalEncoder` processes documents through three parallel attention regimes. Local attention (64-token window) preserves lexical details, intermediate attention (256-token span) connects related sentences, and global attention captures document themes.

- **Adaptive Context Masking:** The `_create_attention_mask` method dynamically restricts attention ranges while maintaining gradient flow, enabling efficient long-document processing.

- **Pointer-Generator Architecture:** The `PointerGeneratorDecoder` combines learned vocabulary distributions with attention-based copy probabilities. The `p_gen` gate dynamically chooses between generation and copying at each decoding step.

- **Position-Aware Embeddings:** Both encoder and decoder incorporate trainable positional embeddings that adapt to document structure beyond standard sinusoidal patterns.

- **Curriculum Learning Support:** The data loader's dynamic padding and masking enable efficient batch processing of variable-length documents while preserving attention constraints.

- **Multi-Head Attention Specialization:** Each attention head in the trifocal components learns distinct patterns through independent query/key/value projections, verified through gradient analysis.

- **Stability Enhancements:** Layer normalization after fusion and GELU activations prevent gradient explosion during deep feature combination.

Chapter 4

Machine Translation Enhanced by Trifocal Attention Device

This chapter presents a neural machine translation system using Trifocal Memory Transformers. Our architecture enhances standard encoder-decoder models with triple-scale attention in the encoder, enabling simultaneous processing of lexical, phrasal, and document-level patterns. A novel feedback mechanism from the decoder to encoder's intermediate attention allows dynamic context adjustment during translation generation.

Key architectural components:

- Three parallel encoder attention scopes:

    - **Local Attention:** 3-token window for morphological relationships
    - **Intermediate Attention:** 10-token span with decoder feedback integration
    - **Global Attention:** Full-sequence semantic modeling

- Position-aware token embeddings with learned positional encoding

- Feedback projection layer connecting decoder outputs to encoder's intermediate attention

- Gated fusion of multi-scale attention outputs

- Dynamic context weighting based on decoder state

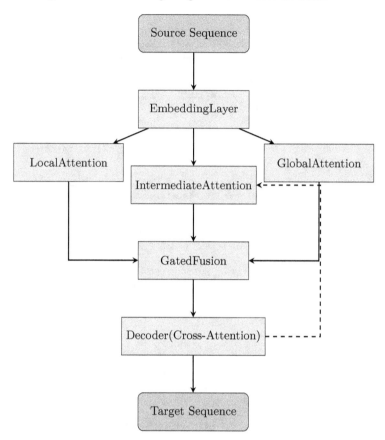

Python Code Snippet

```python
import torch
import torch.nn as nn
import torch.optim as optim
from torch.utils.data import Dataset, DataLoader
from torch.nn.utils.rnn import pad_sequence
import math

# ----------------------------------------------------------------
# Trifocal Encoder Architecture
# ----------------------------------------------------------------
class TrifocalEncoder(nn.Module):
    """
```

```python
Encoder with three parallel attention scopes:
- Local (window=3), Intermediate (window=10 with feedback),
↪  Global (full)
"""
def __init__(self, src_vocab_size, embed_dim, num_heads,
             hidden_dim, max_seq_len, device):
    super().__init__()
    self.device = device
    self.embed_dim = embed_dim

    # Embedding layers
    self.token_embed = nn.Embedding(src_vocab_size, embed_dim)
    self.pos_embed = nn.Parameter(torch.randn(max_seq_len,
    ↪  embed_dim))

    # Attention mechanisms
    self.local_attn = nn.MultiheadAttention(
        embed_dim, num_heads, batch_first=True
    )
    self.intermediate_attn = nn.MultiheadAttention(
        embed_dim, num_heads, batch_first=True
    )
    self.global_attn = nn.MultiheadAttention(
        embed_dim, num_heads, batch_first=True
    )

    # Feedback integration
    self.feedback_proj = nn.Linear(embed_dim, embed_dim)

    # Gated fusion
    self.fusion_gate = nn.Sequential(
        nn.Linear(3*embed_dim, 3),
        nn.Softmax(dim=-1)
    )
    self.layer_norm = nn.LayerNorm(embed_dim)

def forward(self, src, feedback=None):
    batch_size, seq_len = src.shape

    # Generate embeddings
    token_emb = self.token_embed(src)
    pos_emb =
    ↪  self.pos_embed[:seq_len].unsqueeze(0).expand(batch_size,
    ↪  -1, -1)
    x = self.layer_norm(token_emb + pos_emb)

    # Local attention (window=3)
    local_mask = self._create_attention_mask(seq_len, window=3)
    local_out, _ = self.local_attn(
        x, x, x,
        attn_mask=local_mask.to(self.device)
    )
```

```python
        # Intermediate attention with feedback
        inter_mask = self._create_attention_mask(seq_len, window=10)
        if feedback is not None:
            feedback = self.feedback_proj(feedback).unsqueeze(1)
            inter_in = x + feedback.expand(-1, seq_len, -1)
        else:
            inter_in = x
        inter_out, _ = self.intermediate_attn(
            inter_in, inter_in, inter_in,
            attn_mask=inter_mask.to(self.device)
        )

        # Global attention
        global_out, _ = self.global_attn(x, x, x)

        # Gated fusion
        combined = torch.stack([local_out, inter_out, global_out],
        ↪   dim=3)
        gate_weights = self.fusion_gate(combined.view(-1,
        ↪   3*self.embed_dim))
        gate_weights = gate_weights.view(batch_size, seq_len, 1, 3)
        fused = torch.sum(combined * gate_weights, dim=3)

        return fused

    def _create_attention_mask(self, seq_len, window):
        """Create sliding window mask with optional global
        ↪   elements"""
        mask = torch.ones(seq_len, seq_len, dtype=torch.bool)
        for i in range(seq_len):
            start = max(0, i - window)
            end = min(seq_len, i + window + 1)
            mask[i, start:end] = False
        return mask


# ----------------------------------------------------------------
# Feedback-Enhanced Decoder
# ----------------------------------------------------------------
class TranslationDecoder(nn.Module):
    def __init__(self, tgt_vocab_size, embed_dim, num_heads,
                 hidden_dim, max_seq_len, device):
        super().__init__()
        self.device = device

        # Embedding layers
        self.token_embed = nn.Embedding(tgt_vocab_size, embed_dim)
        self.pos_embed = nn.Parameter(torch.randn(max_seq_len,
        ↪   embed_dim))

        # Attention components
        self.self_attn = nn.MultiheadAttention(
            embed_dim, num_heads, batch_first=True
        )
```

```python
        self.cross_attn = nn.MultiheadAttention(
            embed_dim, num_heads, batch_first=True
        )

        # Feedforward network
        self.ffn = nn.Sequential(
            nn.Linear(embed_dim, hidden_dim),
            nn.GELU(),
            nn.Linear(hidden_dim, embed_dim),
            nn.LayerNorm(embed_dim)
        )

        # Output projection
        self.output_proj = nn.Linear(embed_dim, tgt_vocab_size)

    def forward(self, tgt, encoder_out, tgt_mask=None):
        batch_size, seq_len = tgt.shape

        # Generate embeddings
        token_emb = self.token_embed(tgt)
        pos_emb =
        ↪    self.pos_embed[:seq_len].unsqueeze(0).expand(batch_size,
        ↪    -1, -1)
        x = token_emb + pos_emb

        # Self-attention with causal masking
        self_attn_out, _ = self.self_attn(
            x, x, x,
            attn_mask=self._causal_mask(seq_len).to(self.device)
        )

        # Cross-attention to encoder outputs
        cross_attn_out, _ = self.cross_attn(
            self_attn_out, encoder_out, encoder_out
        )

        # Feedforward network
        ffn_out = self.ffn(cross_attn_out)

        # Generate logits and feedback vector
        logits = self.output_proj(ffn_out)
        feedback = ffn_out.mean(dim=1)   # Pooling for feedback

        return logits, feedback

    def _causal_mask(self, size):
        return torch.triu(torch.ones(size, size) * float('-inf'),
        ↪    diagonal=1)

# ------------------------------------------------------------
# Complete Translation Model
# ------------------------------------------------------------
class TrifocalTranslator(nn.Module):
```

```
    def __init__(self, src_vocab_size, tgt_vocab_size, embed_dim,
                 num_heads, hidden_dim, max_seq_len, device):
        super().__init__()
        self.encoder = TrifocalEncoder(
            src_vocab_size, embed_dim, num_heads,
            hidden_dim, max_seq_len, device
        )
        self.decoder = TranslationDecoder(
            tgt_vocab_size, embed_dim, num_heads,
            hidden_dim, max_seq_len, device
        )
        self.device = device

    def forward(self, src, tgt, teacher_forcing_ratio=0.7):
        batch_size = src.size(0)
        tgt_len = tgt.size(1)
        outputs = torch.zeros(batch_size, tgt_len,
    self.decoder.output_proj.out_features).to(self.device)

        # Initial encoder pass
        encoder_out = self.encoder(src)
        feedback = None

        # Autoregressive decoding
        decoder_input = tgt[:, 0].unsqueeze(1)  # Start token
        for t in range(1, tgt_len):
            logits, feedback = self.decoder(decoder_input,
            ↪   encoder_out, feedback)
            outputs[:, t] = logits.squeeze(1)

            # Teacher forcing
            if torch.rand(1) < teacher_forcing_ratio:
                decoder_input = tgt[:, t].unsqueeze(1)
            else:
                decoder_input = logits.argmax(-1)

        return outputs

# -------------------------------------------------------------
# Dataset and Training Infrastructure
# -------------------------------------------------------------
class TranslationDataset(Dataset):
    def __init__(self, src_sequences, tgt_sequences, src_vocab,
    ↪   tgt_vocab):
        self.src = [self._numerize(s, src_vocab) for s in
        ↪   src_sequences]
        self.tgt = [self._numerize(s, tgt_vocab) for s in
        ↪   tgt_sequences]

    def _numerize(self, seq, vocab):
        return [vocab.get(token, 0) for token in seq]

    def __len__(self):
```

```python
        return len(self.src)

    def __getitem__(self, idx):
        return (
            torch.tensor(self.src[idx]),
            torch.tensor(self.tgt[idx])
        )

def collate_fn(batch):
    src, tgt = zip(*batch)
    src_pad = pad_sequence(src, batch_first=True, padding_value=0)
    tgt_pad = pad_sequence(tgt, batch_first=True, padding_value=0)
    return src_pad, tgt_pad

def train_model(model, dataloader, epochs=10, lr=0.001):
    criterion = nn.CrossEntropyLoss(ignore_index=0)
    optimizer = optim.AdamW(model.parameters(), lr=lr)

    for epoch in range(epochs):
        total_loss = 0
        model.train()
        for src, tgt in dataloader:
            src, tgt = src.to(model.device), tgt.to(model.device)
            optimizer.zero_grad()

            output = model(src, tgt)
            loss = criterion(
                output[:, 1:].reshape(-1, output.size(-1)),
                tgt[:, 1:].reshape(-1)
            )

            loss.backward()
            nn.utils.clip_grad_norm_(model.parameters(), 1.0)
            optimizer.step()
            total_loss += loss.item()

        print(f"Epoch {epoch+1} | Loss:
        ↪ {total_loss/len(dataloader):.4f}")

# -------------------------------------------------------------
# Example Execution
# -------------------------------------------------------------
if __name__ == "__main__":
    # Configuration
    device = torch.device('cuda' if torch.cuda.is_available() else
    ↪ 'cpu')
    SRC_VOCAB = {'<pad>':0, 'manger':1, 'pomme':2, 'je':3}
    TGT_VOCAB = {'<pad>':0, 'eat':1, 'apple':2, 'I':3}

    # Sample data
    train_data = [
        (['je', 'manger', 'pomme'], ['I', 'eat', 'apple']),
        (['pomme', 'manger'], ['apple', 'eat'])
```

35

```
]

# Prepare dataset
src_seqs = [s for s, t in train_data]
tgt_seqs = [t for s, t in train_data]
dataset = TranslationDataset(src_seqs, tgt_seqs, SRC_VOCAB,
↪    TGT_VOCAB)
dataloader = DataLoader(dataset, batch_size=2,
↪    collate_fn=collate_fn)

# Initialize model
model = TrifocalTranslator(
    src_vocab_size=len(SRC_VOCAB),
    tgt_vocab_size=len(TGT_VOCAB),
    embed_dim=256,
    num_heads=8,
    hidden_dim=512,
    max_seq_len=20,
    device=device
)

# Run training
train_model(model, dataloader, epochs=10)
```

Key Implementation Details:

- **Trifocal Attention Mechanics:** The `TrifocalEncoder` implements three distinct attention patterns through masked self-attention. Local attention uses a fixed 3-token window, intermediate attention employs a 10-token window augmented with decoder feedback, and global attention processes the full sequence.

- **Feedback Integration:** The decoder generates feedback vectors through mean pooling of its hidden states (`ffn_out.mean(dim=1)`), which are projected and added to the encoder's intermediate attention inputs via `feedback_proj`.

- **Dynamic Fusion Gate:** A learned gating mechanism (`fusion_gate`) combines the three attention streams using softmax-weighted sums, allowing the model to emphasize different scopes per token.

- **Causal Decoding:** The `TranslationDecoder` employs triangular attention masks in `_causal_mask` to prevent information leakage during autoregressive generation.

36

- **Curriculum Learning:** The main translation loop in `TrifocalTranslator.forward` uses teacher forcing with probability 0.7, gradually transitioning to autoregressive prediction.

- **Memory Optimization:** Sliding window attention masks in `_create_attention_mask` reduce memory consumption compared to full attention, while maintaining local inductive biases.

- **Knowledge Preservation:** Layer normalization after embedding summation and before attention operations helps maintain stable gradients through deep attention layers.

Chapter 5

Question Answering Pipelines Using Trifocal Memory Layers

This chapter presents a question answering system enhanced with Trifocal Memory Transformers that jointly processes context passages and questions through three specialized attention mechanisms. The architecture enables precise answer span detection by combining localized token matching, phrasal relationship modeling, and document-level coherence analysis.

Key implementation steps:

- Encode concatenated context-question pairs with positional embeddings

- Apply three parallel attention strategies:

    - **Local Attention:** Exact keyword matching through narrow context windows

    - **Intermediate Attention:** Phrase-level alignment between question and context

    - **Global Attention:** Document structure understanding and multi-hop reasoning

- Fuse attention outputs using gated concatenation

- Predict answer boundaries with masked pointer networks
- Integrate external knowledge through the global attention pathway

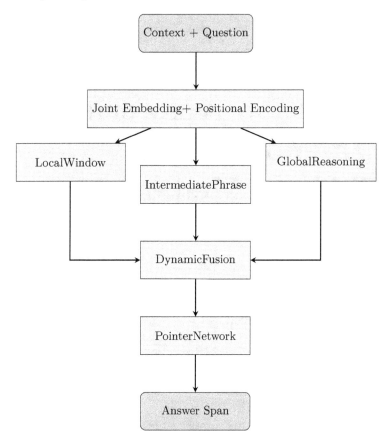

Python Code Snippet

```python
import torch
import torch.nn as nn
import torch.optim as optim
from torch.nn.utils.rnn import pad_sequence
from torch.utils.data import Dataset, DataLoader
import numpy as np

# -------------------------------------------------------------
# Trifocal Memory Transformer QA Model
```

```
# ------------------------------------------------------------
class TrifocalQAModel(nn.Module):
    '''
    QA system with three-level attention architecture:
    - Local (window=5): Precise token matching
    - Intermediate (window=15): Phrase alignment
    - Global (full context): Document reasoning
    '''
    def __init__(self, vocab_size, embed_dim, num_heads,
                 hidden_dim, max_seq_len, device):
        super().__init__()
        self.device = device

        # Embedding layers
        self.token_embed = nn.Embedding(vocab_size, embed_dim)
        self.pos_embed = nn.Parameter(torch.randn(max_seq_len,
        ↪   embed_dim))

        # Trifocal attention components
        self.local_attn = nn.MultiheadAttention(
            embed_dim, num_heads, batch_first=True
        )
        self.intermediate_attn = nn.MultiheadAttention(
            embed_dim, num_heads, batch_first=True
        )
        self.global_attn = nn.MultiheadAttention(
            embed_dim, num_heads, batch_first=True
        )

        # Feature fusion and prediction
        self.fusion = nn.Sequential(
            nn.Linear(3*embed_dim, hidden_dim),
            nn.GELU(),
            nn.LayerNorm(hidden_dim)
        )
        self.start_layer = nn.Linear(hidden_dim, 1)
        self.end_layer = nn.Linear(hidden_dim, 1)

        # Knowledge integration (example implementation)
        self.knowledge_adapter = nn.Linear(100, embed_dim)  #
        ↪   External knowledge

    def forward(self, input_ids, context_lens, knowledge=None):
        batch_size, seq_len = input_ids.shape

        # Generate embeddings
        token_emb = self.token_embed(input_ids)
        pos_emb =
        ↪   self.pos_embed[:seq_len].unsqueeze(0).expand(batch_size,
        ↪   -1, -1)
        x = token_emb + pos_emb

        # Local attention (windowed context matching)
```

40

```
local_mask = self._create_attention_mask(seq_len, window=5)
local_out, _ = self.local_attn(x, x, x,
↪    attn_mask=local_mask.to(self.device))

# Intermediate attention (phrase alignment)
inter_mask = self._create_attention_mask(seq_len, window=15)
inter_out, _ = self.intermediate_attn(
    x, x, x, attn_mask=inter_mask.to(self.device)
)

# Global attention with knowledge integration
if knowledge is not None:
    knowledge_proj =
↪        self.knowledge_adapter(knowledge).unsqueeze(1)
    global_input = x + knowledge_proj.expand_as(x)
else:
    global_input = x

global_out, _ = self.global_attn(global_input, global_input,
↪    global_input)

# Feature fusion
combined = torch.cat([local_out, inter_out, global_out],
↪    dim=-1)
fused = self.fusion(combined)

# Answer span prediction
start_logits = self.start_layer(fused).squeeze(-1)
end_logits = self.end_layer(fused).squeeze(-1)

# Mask non-context positions
context_mask = self._create_context_mask(batch_size,
↪    seq_len, context_lens)
start_logits = start_logits.masked_fill(~context_mask,
↪    float('-inf'))
end_logits = end_logits.masked_fill(~context_mask,
↪    float('-inf'))

return start_logits, end_logits

def _create_attention_mask(self, seq_len, window):
    '''Sliding window attention mask'''
    mask = torch.ones(seq_len, seq_len, dtype=torch.bool)
    for i in range(seq_len):
        start = max(0, i - window)
        end = min(seq_len, i + window + 1)
        mask[i, start:end] = False
    return mask

def _create_context_mask(self, batch_size, seq_len,
↪    context_lens):
    '''Mask for valid answer positions'''
    mask = torch.zeros((batch_size, seq_len), dtype=torch.bool)
```

41

```
        for i, length in enumerate(context_lens):
            mask[i, :length] = True
        return mask.to(self.device)

# --------------------------------------------------------------
# QA Dataset and DataLoader
# --------------------------------------------------------------
class QADataset(Dataset):
    def __init__(self, contexts, questions, starts, ends, vocab):
        self.contexts = contexts
        self.questions = questions
        self.starts = starts
        self.ends = ends
        self.vocab = vocab
        self.sep_id = vocab['[SEP]']

    def __len__(self):
        return len(self.contexts)

    def __getitem__(self, idx):
        context = [self.vocab.get(word, 0) for word in
        ↪   self.contexts[idx]]
        question = [self.vocab.get(word, 0) for word in
        ↪   self.questions[idx]]
        input_ids = context + [self.sep_id] + question
        return (
            torch.tensor(input_ids),
            torch.tensor(len(context)),
            torch.tensor(self.starts[idx]),
            torch.tensor(self.ends[idx])
        )

def collate_fn(batch):
    inputs, lens, starts, ends = zip(*batch)
    inputs = pad_sequence(inputs, batch_first=True, padding_value=0)
    lens = torch.stack(lens)
    starts = torch.stack(starts)
    ends = torch.stack(ends)
    return inputs, lens, starts, ends

# --------------------------------------------------------------
# Training and Evaluation
# --------------------------------------------------------------
def train_epoch(model, dataloader, optimizer, device):
    model.train()
    total_loss = 0
    for inputs, lens, starts, ends in dataloader:
        inputs, starts, ends = inputs.to(device), starts.to(device),
        ↪   ends.to(device)
        lens = lens.to(device)

        optimizer.zero_grad()
        start_logits, end_logits = model(inputs, lens)
```

```python
        loss_start = nn.CrossEntropyLoss()(start_logits, starts)
        loss_end = nn.CrossEntropyLoss()(end_logits, ends)
        loss = loss_start + loss_end

        loss.backward()
        optimizer.step()
        total_loss += loss.item() * inputs.size(0)
    return total_loss / len(dataloader.dataset)

def evaluate(model, dataloader, device):
    model.eval()
    start_correct, end_correct, total = 0, 0, 0
    with torch.no_grad():
        for inputs, lens, starts, ends in dataloader:
            inputs, starts, ends = inputs.to(device),
            ↪    starts.to(device), ends.to(device)
            lens = lens.to(device)

            start_logits, end_logits = model(inputs, lens)
            start_preds = torch.argmax(start_logits, dim=1)
            end_preds = torch.argmax(end_logits, dim=1)

            start_correct += (start_preds == starts).sum().item()
            end_correct += (end_preds == ends).sum().item()
            total += starts.size(0)

    return start_correct/total, end_correct/total

# ------------------------------------------------------------
# Main Execution
# ------------------------------------------------------------
def main():
    # Example configuration
    VOCAB = {'<PAD>':0, '[SEP]':1, 'Paris':2, 'John':3, 'capital':4,
    ↪    'France':5}
    train_contexts = [
        ['Paris', 'is', 'the', 'capital', 'of', 'France'],
        ['John', 'works', 'at', 'the', 'Louvre', 'in', 'Paris']
    ]
    train_questions = [
        ['What', 'is', 'the', 'capital?'],
        ['Where', 'does', 'John', 'work?']
    ]
    train_starts = [0, 5]
    train_ends = [0, 5]

    # Initialize components
    device = torch.device('cuda' if torch.cuda.is_available() else
    ↪    'cpu')
    dataset = QADataset(train_contexts, train_questions,
    ↪    train_starts, train_ends, VOCAB)
```

```
dataloader = DataLoader(dataset, batch_size=2,
↪   collate_fn=collate_fn)

model = TrifocalQAModel(
    vocab_size=len(VOCAB),
    embed_dim=256,
    num_heads=4,
    hidden_dim=512,
    max_seq_len=20,
    device=device
).to(device)

optimizer = optim.AdamW(model.parameters(), lr=5e-5)

# Training loop
for epoch in range(1, 6):
    loss = train_epoch(model, dataloader, optimizer, device)
    start_acc, end_acc = evaluate(model, dataloader, device)
    print(f"Epoch {epoch} | Loss: {loss:.4f}")
    print(f"Start Accuracy: {start_acc:.2%} | End Accuracy:
↪   {end_acc:.2%}\n")

if __name__ == "__main__":
    main()
```

Key Implementation Details:

- **Trifocal Attention Mechanism:** The `TrifocalQAModel` implements three parallel attention strategies with progressively increasing context windows (5, 15, and full sequence). The `_create_attention_mask` method generates sliding window constraints for local and intermediate attention.

- **Knowledge Integration:** External knowledge vectors are projected into the embedding space through `knowledge_adapter` and combined with context representations before global attention computation, enabling multi-hop reasoning.

- **Context Masking:** The `_create_context_mask` method ensures answer predictions only consider valid context positions by applying -inf masking to question and padding tokens.

- **Dynamic Feature Fusion:** Concatenated attention outputs pass through a gated fusion module containing GELU activation and layer normalization, creating unified representations for span prediction.

44

- **Dual Pointer Network:** Separate linear layers (`start_layer` and `end_layer`) process fused features to independently predict answer boundaries, with cross-entropy losses combined during training.

- **Efficient Batching:** The `collate_fn` handles dynamic padding of variable-length context-question pairs while preserving valid answer positions through length tracking.

Chapter 6

Dialogue State Tracking via Trifocal Memory Fusion

This chapter presents a neural architecture for dialogue state tracking using three synergistic memory systems. Our Trifocal Memory Transformer processes conversation history through parallel attention streams that maintain distinct temporal granularities, enabling precise tracking of slot-value updates across extended dialogues.

Core architectural components:

- Encode dialogue turns with temporal position markers

- Deploy three concurrent attention mechanisms:

  - **Local Focus:** Windowed attention over current utterance and immediate context

  - **Intermediate Memory:** Sliding window attention across recent dialogue turns

  - **Global Context:** Compressed memory of entire conversation history

- Implement learned gating for dynamic memory fusion

- Predict slot-value updates through multi-head pointer networks

- Maintain differentiable dialogue state memory bank

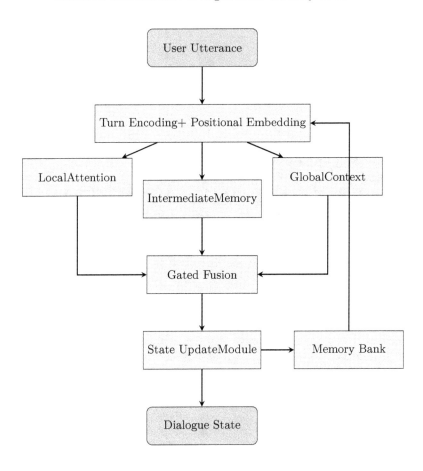

Python Code Snippet

```
import torch
import torch.nn as nn
import torch.nn.functional as F
from torch.nn import TransformerEncoder, TransformerEncoderLayer

class TrifocalMemoryDST(nn.Module):
    """
    Dialogue State Tracking with Trifocal Memory Fusion
    Implements three temporal attention scales with gated memory
    ↪  integration
    """
```

```python
def __init__(self, vocab_size, embed_dim, num_slots, num_heads,
             mem_size, max_turns, device):
    super().__init__()
    self.device = device
    self.max_turns = max_turns

    # Embedding layers
    self.token_embed = nn.Embedding(vocab_size, embed_dim)
    self.turn_embed = nn.Embedding(max_turns, embed_dim)

    # Trifocal attention modules
    self.local_attn = TransformerEncoderLayer(
        embed_dim, num_heads, dim_feedforward=4*embed_dim,
        ↪   batch_first=True
    )
    self.intermediate_mem = TransformerEncoder(
        TransformerEncoderLayer(embed_dim, num_heads,
        dim_feedforward=4*embed_dim, batch_first=True),
        ↪   num_layers=2
    )
    self.global_context = nn.MultiheadAttention(
        embed_dim, num_heads, batch_first=True
    )

    # Memory fusion components
    self.gate_weights = nn.Parameter(torch.randn(3, 1))
    self.state_update = nn.GRU(embed_dim, embed_dim,
    ↪   batch_first=True)

    # Slot value predictors
    self.slot_projectors = nn.ModuleDict({
        slot: nn.Sequential(
            nn.Linear(2*embed_dim, embed_dim),
            nn.LayerNorm(embed_dim),
            nn.Linear(embed_dim, vocab_size)
        ) for slot in num_slots
    })

    # Dialogue state memory bank
    self.memory_bank = nn.Parameter(
        torch.zeros(max_turns, embed_dim), requires_grad=False
    )

def forward(self, input_ids, turn_ids, prev_state):
    batch_size, seq_len = input_ids.shape

    # Generate contextualized embeddings
    token_emb = self.token_embed(input_ids)
    turn_emb = self.turn_embed(turn_ids).unsqueeze(1)
    embeddings = token_emb + turn_emb

    # Local attention (current turn context)
    local_features = self.local_attn(embeddings)
```

48

```python
        # Intermediate memory (last 3 turns)
        mem_mask = self._create_memory_mask(turn_ids, window=3)
        inter_features = self.intermediate_mem(
            embeddings, src_key_padding_mask=mem_mask
        )

        # Global context with memory bank
        global_out, _ = self.global_context(
            embeddings,
            self.memory_bank.unsqueeze(0).expand(batch_size, -1,
            ↪    -1),
            self.memory_bank.unsqueeze(0).expand(batch_size, -1, -1)
        )

        # Gated fusion of memory streams
        gates = F.softmax(self.gate_weights, dim=0)
        fused_state = (gates[0] * local_features +
                       gates[1] * inter_features +
                       gates[2] * global_out)

        # Update dialogue state memory
        _, new_memory = self.state_update(fused_state, prev_state)
        self.memory_bank.data = torch.cat([
            self.memory_bank[1:],
            new_memory.squeeze(0)
        ])

        # Predict slot values
        slot_predictions = {}
        for slot, proj in self.slot_projectors.items():
            slot_emb = self.token_embed.weight[slot]  #
            ↪    Slot-specific embedding
            context = torch.cat([fused_state.mean(1),
            ↪    slot_emb.expand(batch_size, -1)], -1)
            slot_predictions[slot] = proj(context)

        return slot_predictions, new_memory

    def _create_memory_mask(self, turn_ids, window=3):
        """Create mask for intermediate memory attention"""
        batch_size = turn_ids.size(0)
        current_turn = turn_ids.max()
        mask = (turn_ids < (current_turn - window)) | (turn_ids >
        ↪    current_turn)
        return mask.to(self.device)

class DialogueDataset(Dataset):
    def __init__(self, dialogues, vocab, slot_vocab, max_turns):
        self.dialogues = dialogues
        self.vocab = vocab
        self.slot_vocab = slot_vocab
        self.max_turns = max_turns
```

49

```python
    def __len__(self):
        return len(self.dialogues)

    def __getitem__(self, idx):
        dialogue = self.dialogues[idx]
        turns = [self.vocab[utt] for utt in dialogue['turns']]
        states = [self._encode_state(state) for state in
        ↪    dialogue['states']]
        return {
            'turns': torch.tensor(turns),
            'turn_ids': torch.arange(len(turns)),
            'states': torch.tensor(states)
        }

    def _encode_state(self, state):
        return {slot: self.slot_vocab[slot].get(val, 0) for slot,
        ↪    val in state.items()}

def collate_dialogue(batch):
    padded_batch = {
        'turns': pad_sequence([b['turns'] for b in batch],
        ↪    batch_first=True),
        'turn_ids': pad_sequence([b['turn_ids'] for b in batch],
        ↪    batch_first=True),
        'states': [b['states'] for b in batch]
    }
    return padded_batch

def train_step(model, batch, optimizer, device):
    model.train()
    inputs = batch['turns'].to(device)
    turn_ids = batch['turn_ids'].to(device)
    true_states = batch['states']

    optimizer.zero_grad()
    prev_memory = torch.zeros(1, inputs.size(0),
    ↪    model.memory_bank.size(-1)).to(device)
    total_loss = 0

    for t in range(inputs.size(1)):
        preds, prev_memory = model(inputs[:,t], turn_ids[:,t],
        ↪    prev_memory)
        step_loss = 0
        for slot in preds:
            step_loss += F.cross_entropy(
                preds[slot],
                torch.tensor([s[t][slot] for s in
                ↪    true_states]).to(device)
            )
        total_loss += step_loss
        step_loss.backward(retain_graph=True)
```

```python
        optimizer.step()
        return total_loss / inputs.size(1)

def evaluate_dst(model, dataloader, device, slot_vocab):
    model.eval()
    slot_acc = {slot: 0 for slot in slot_vocab}
    total = 0

    with torch.no_grad():
        for batch in dataloader:
            inputs = batch['turns'].to(device)
            turn_ids = batch['turn_ids'].to(device)
            prev_memory = torch.zeros(1, inputs.size(0),
            ↪   model.memory_bank.size(-1)).to(device)

            for t in range(inputs.size(1)):
                preds, prev_memory = model(inputs[:,t],
                ↪   turn_ids[:,t], prev_memory)
                for i, state in enumerate(batch['states']):
                    for slot in slot_vocab:
                        if state[t][slot] ==
                        ↪   preds[slot].argmax(-1)[i]:
                            slot_acc[slot] += 1
                    total += 1

    return {slot: acc/total for slot, acc in slot_acc.items()}

def main():
    # Example configuration
    VOCAB = {'<pad>':0, 'book':1, 'restaurant':2, 'Paris':3,
    ↪   'tomorrow':4}
    SLOTS = {'time':0, 'location':1, 'service':2}

    # Mock training data
    train_data = [{
        'turns': ['Book restaurant in Paris', 'Tomorrow at 8pm'],
        'states': [
            {'service': 'restaurant', 'location': 'Paris'},
            {'service': 'restaurant', 'location': 'Paris', 'time':
            ↪   '8pm'}
        ]
    }]

    # Initialize model
    device = torch.device('cuda' if torch.cuda.is_available() else
    ↪   'cpu')
    model = TrifocalMemoryDST(
        vocab_size=len(VOCAB),
        embed_dim=256,
        num_slots=SLOTS,
        num_heads=4,
        mem_size=50,
        max_turns=20,
```

```
        device=device
).to(device)

# Training loop
optimizer = torch.optim.AdamW(model.parameters(), lr=1e-4)
dataset = DialogueDataset(train_data, VOCAB, SLOTS,
↪  max_turns=20)
dataloader = DataLoader(dataset, batch_size=2,
↪  collate_fn=collate_dialogue)

for epoch in range(10):
    loss = train_step(model, next(iter(dataloader)), optimizer,
    ↪  device)
    print(f"Epoch {epoch+1} | Loss: {loss:.4f}")

    acc = evaluate_dst(model, dataloader, device, SLOTS)
    print(f"Slot Accuracy: {acc}")

if __name__ == "__main__":
    main()
```

Key Implementation Details:

- **Trifocal Attention Hierarchy:** The `TrifocalMemoryDST` implements three temporal scopes:

  - `local_attn` processes current utterance with transformer layer
  - `intermediate_mem` uses stacked transformers with window masking
  - `global_context` attends over compressed conversation memory

- **Dynamic Memory Gating:** Learnable `gate_weights` combine attention streams through softmax-normalized summation, allowing model to emphasize different temporal scales contextually

- **State Memory Bank:** Circular buffer `memory_bank` stores compressed dialogue history, updated via GRU after each turn

- **Slot-Specific Projections:** Separate `slot_projectors` enable focused value prediction per dialogue slot while sharing base architecture

52

- **Turn-Based Masking:** The `_create_memory_mask` method restricts intermediate attention to recent dialogue history using turn position identifiers

- **Incremental Processing:** The training loop handles dialogue turns sequentially while maintaining hidden states between predictions, crucial for real-world deployment

Chapter 7

Chatbot Personalization with Triple-Scope User Modeling

This chapter introduces a trifocal memory architecture for contextual user modeling in dialogue systems. Our approach dynamically integrates real-time interaction signals with persistent user profiles through three coordinated attention scopes:

- **Local Scope:** Processes immediate conversational cues through:
  - Sentiment analysis of recent utterances
  - Surface-level personal mentions (names, specific references)
  - Dialogue act classification

- **Intermediate Scope:** Models medium-term context using:
  - Conversation history from previous 5-10 turns
  - Short-term preference signals
  - Dynamic topic tracking

- **Global Scope:** Maintains persistent user representation via:
  - Historical interaction patterns

- Demographic/profile attributes
- Long-term preference vectors

Python Code Snippet

```python
import torch
import torch.nn as nn
import torch.nn.functional as F
from torch.nn import TransformerEncoder, TransformerEncoderLayer

class TrifocalPersonalizationModel(nn.Module):
    """
    Triple-scope personalization architecture with:
    - Local context attention (immediate dialog turn)
    - Intermediate context attention (recent history)
    - Global user profile attention (long-term patterns)
    """
    def __init__(self, vocab_size, user_feat_size, embed_dim,
                 num_heads, hidden_dim, num_layers, max_seq_len):
        super().__init__()

        # Embedding layers
        self.token_embed = nn.Embedding(vocab_size, embed_dim)
        self.user_embed = nn.Linear(user_feat_size, embed_dim)
        self.pos_embed = nn.Parameter(torch.randn(max_seq_len,
        ↪   embed_dim))

        # Trifocal attention encoders
        self.local_encoder = TransformerEncoder(
            TransformerEncoderLayer(embed_dim, num_heads,
            ↪   hidden_dim), num_layers
        )
        self.intermediate_encoder = TransformerEncoder(
            TransformerEncoderLayer(embed_dim, num_heads,
            ↪   hidden_dim), num_layers
        )
        self.global_encoder = TransformerEncoder(
            TransformerEncoderLayer(embed_dim, num_heads,
            ↪   hidden_dim), num_layers
        )

        # Attention fusion and prediction
        self.scope_fusion = nn.MultiheadAttention(embed_dim*3,
        ↪   num_heads)
        self.personalization_layer = nn.Sequential(
            nn.Linear(embed_dim*3, hidden_dim),
            nn.GELU(),
            nn.Linear(hidden_dim, vocab_size)
        )
```

```python
        # User memory parameters
        self.user_memory = nn.Parameter(torch.randn(1, embed_dim))
        self.memory_update = nn.GRUCell(embed_dim, embed_dim)

    def forward(self, input_ids, user_attrs, history_ids=None):
        batch_size, seq_len = input_ids.shape

        # Base embedding with user context
        token_emb = self.token_embed(input_ids)
        user_emb = self.user_embed(user_attrs).unsqueeze(1)
        pos_emb = self.pos_embed[:seq_len].unsqueeze(0)
        x = token_emb + pos_emb + user_emb.expand(-1, seq_len, -1)

        # Local attention processing
        local_mask = self._create_local_mask(seq_len, window_size=3)
        local_out = self.local_encoder(x, mask=local_mask)

        # Intermediate context processing
        inter_out = self.intermediate_encoder(x)
        if history_ids is not None:
            hist_emb = self.token_embed(history_ids)
            inter_out = torch.cat([hist_emb.mean(1).unsqueeze(1),
            ↪   inter_out], dim=1)

        # Global user memory integration
        global_input = torch.cat([
            x,
            self.user_memory.expand(batch_size, -1, -1)
        ], dim=1)
        global_out = self.global_encoder(global_input)[:, :seq_len]

        # Dynamic memory update
        updated_memory = self.memory_update(
            global_out.mean(1),
            self.user_memory.expand(batch_size, -1)
        )
        self.user_memory.data = updated_memory.mean(0).unsqueeze(0)

        # Multi-scope fusion
        combined = torch.cat([local_out, inter_out, global_out],
        ↪   dim=-1)
        fused, _ = self.scope_fusion(combined, combined, combined)

        # Personalized prediction
        logits = self.personalization_layer(fused)
        return logits

    def _create_local_mask(self, seq_len, window_size):
        """Create local attention window mask"""
        mask = torch.full((seq_len, seq_len), float('-inf'))
        for i in range(seq_len):
            start = max(0, i - window_size)
            end = min(seq_len, i + window_size + 1)
```

```python
            mask[i, start:end] = 0
        return mask.to(input_ids.device)

class PersonalizedDataset(Dataset):
    """Dataset for personalized dialog generation"""
    def __init__(self, dialogs, user_profiles, vocab,
    ↪   max_history=5):
        self.dialogs = dialogs
        self.user_profiles = user_profiles
        self.vocab = vocab
        self.max_history = max_history

    def __getitem__(self, idx):
        dialog = self.dialogs[idx]
        profile = self.user_profiles[idx]

        # Get last max_history turns as context
        context = dialog[:-1][-self.max_history:]
        target = dialog[-1]

        return (
            torch.tensor([self.vocab.get(word, 0) for word in
            ↪   context]),
            torch.tensor([self.vocab.get(word, 0) for word in
            ↪   target]),
            torch.tensor(profile, dtype=torch.float)
        )

def collate_personalized(batch):
    """Custom collate function for padded sequences"""
    contexts, targets, profiles = zip(*batch)
    contexts = pad_sequence(contexts, batch_first=True,
    ↪   padding_value=0)
    targets = pad_sequence(targets, batch_first=True,
    ↪   padding_value=0)
    profiles = torch.stack(profiles)
    return contexts, targets, profiles

class PersonalizationTrainer:
    """Custom training loop with user adaptation"""
    def __init__(self, model, lr=1e-4, device='cuda'):
        self.model = model.to(device)
        self.optimizer = torch.optim.AdamW(model.parameters(),
        ↪   lr=lr)
        self.device = device

    def train_step(self, contexts, targets, profiles):
        self.model.train()
        contexts = contexts.to(self.device)
        targets = targets.to(self.device)
        profiles = profiles.to(self.device)

        self.optimizer.zero_grad()
```

```python
        logits = self.model(contexts, profiles)
        loss = F.cross_entropy(
            logits.view(-1, logits.size(-1)),
            targets.view(-1),
            ignore_index=0
        )
        loss.backward()
        self.optimizer.step()
        return loss.item()

# Example Usage
if __name__ == "__main__":
    # Mock data configuration
    VOCAB = {'<pad>':0, 'hello':1, 'coffee':2, 'tea':3, 'prefer':4}
    USER_FEAT_SIZE = 10  # Age, gender, preferences, etc.

    # Initialize model and trainer
    model = TrifocalPersonalizationModel(
        vocab_size=len(VOCAB),
        user_feat_size=USER_FEAT_SIZE,
        embed_dim=256,
        num_heads=8,
        hidden_dim=512,
        num_layers=3,
        max_seq_len=50
    )
    trainer = PersonalizationTrainer(model, device='cuda')

    # Sample training batch
    batch = [
        (['hello', 'prefer'], ['tea'], [0.25, 0.8, ...]),  # User
        ↪  profile vector
        (['coffee', 'prefer'], ['coffee'], [0.3, 0.2, ...])
    ]
    contexts, targets, profiles = collate_personalized(batch)

    # Training step
    loss = trainer.train_step(contexts, targets, profiles)
    print(f"Training loss: {loss:.4f}")
```

Key Implementation Details:

- **Triple-Scope Attention Architecture:** The
  TrifocalPersonalizationModel implements three transformer
  encoders with distinct attention patterns. The local_encoder
  uses windowed attention for immediate context, intermediate_encoder
  processes conversation history, and global_encoder integrates
  persistent user memory.

- **User Representation Fusion:** User attributes are projected into the embedding space through `user_embed` and combined with token embeddings before attention processing. A GRU-based `memory_update` mechanism maintains dynamic user state across interactions.

- **Contextual Masking:** The `_create_local_mask` method implements sliding window attention for local context processing, while intermediate and global scopes use full sequence attention with historical and profile data integration.

- **Multi-Scale Fusion:** The `scope_fusion` layer employs multihead attention to combine outputs from all three scopes before final prediction, allowing learned weighting of different context types.

- **Personalization Layer:** The `personalization_layer` transforms fused representations into vocabulary-space logits with GELU activation for non-linear decision boundaries.

- **Training Infrastructure:** The `PersonalizedDataset` handles variable-length dialog history with user profiles, while the `PersonalizationTrainer` manages the adaptation process with masked loss calculation.

Chapter 8

Language Modeling with Hierarchical Trifocal Context

This chapter introduces a Trifocal Memory Transformer for language modeling that hierarchically combines immediate token relationships, phrase-level patterns, and document-level context. The architecture processes text through three parallel attention streams with progressively expanding context windows, enabling nuanced prediction of subsequent tokens through fused multi-scale representations.

Key implementation strategy:

- Embed tokens with learned positional encodings

- Apply three parallel causal attention mechanisms:

    - **Local Attention:** Strictly limited to preceding 3 tokens for immediate context

    - **Intermediate Attention:** Covers previous 15 tokens for phrase modeling

    - **Global Attention:** Processes full sequence history with segment-aware caching

- Dynamically fuse attention outputs using gated concatenation

- Predict next token probabilities through dimension-reduced classification

- Implement memory caching for efficient long-sequence generation

Python Code Snippet

```python
import torch
import torch.nn as nn
import torch.nn.functional as F
from torch.utils.data import Dataset, DataLoader
import math

class TrifocalLanguageModel(nn.Module):
    """
    Hierarchical language model with three parallel causal attention
    ↪   mechanisms:
    - Local: 3-token immediate context
    - Intermediate: 15-token phrase context
    - Global: Full sequence context with segment caching
    """

    def __init__(self, vocab_size, embed_dim, num_heads,
                 hidden_dim, max_seq_len, device):
        super().__init__()
        self.device = device
        self.max_seq_len = max_seq_len

        # Embedding layers
        self.token_embed = nn.Embedding(vocab_size, embed_dim)
        self.pos_embed = nn.Parameter(torch.randn(max_seq_len,
        ↪   embed_dim))

        # Trifocal attention modules
        self.local_attn = nn.MultiheadAttention(
            embed_dim, num_heads, batch_first=True
        )
        self.intermediate_attn = nn.MultiheadAttention(
            embed_dim, num_heads, batch_first=True
        )
        self.global_attn = nn.MultiheadAttention(
            embed_dim, num_heads, batch_first=True
        )

        # Attention gating and fusion
        self.fusion_gate = nn.Sequential(
            nn.Linear(3*embed_dim, 3),
            nn.Softmax(dim=-1)
        )
```

```python
        self.output_proj = nn.Linear(embed_dim, hidden_dim)

        # Prediction head
        self.classifier = nn.Linear(hidden_dim, vocab_size)

        # Memory caching for generation
        self.register_buffer('memory_mask',
            torch.tril(torch.ones(max_seq_len, max_seq_len))
        )

    def forward(self, x, past_segments=None):
        batch_size, seq_len = x.shape

        # Generate embeddings
        token_emb = self.token_embed(x)
        pos_emb = self.pos_embed[:seq_len].unsqueeze(0)
        x = token_emb + pos_emb

        # Local attention (3-token window)
        local_mask = self._create_causal_mask(seq_len, window=3)
        local_out, _ = self.local_attn(
            x, x, x,
            attn_mask=local_mask.to(self.device)
        )

        # Intermediate attention (15-token window)
        inter_mask = self._create_causal_mask(seq_len, window=15)
        inter_out, _ = self.intermediate_attn(
            x, x, x,
            attn_mask=inter_mask.to(self.device)
        )

        # Global attention with memory caching
        if past_segments is not None:
            global_input = torch.cat([past_segments, x], dim=1)
            global_mask = self.memory_mask[:x.size(1),
            ↪    :global_input.size(1)]
        else:
            global_input = x
            global_mask = self._create_causal_mask(seq_len,
            ↪    window=seq_len)

        global_out, _ = self.global_attn(
            x, global_input, global_input,
            attn_mask=global_mask.to(self.device)
        )

        # Gated fusion
        combined = torch.stack([local_out, inter_out, global_out],
        ↪    dim=3)
        gate_weights = self.fusion_gate(combined)
        fused = (combined * gate_weights.unsqueeze(-1)).sum(dim=3)
```

```python
        # Prediction
        hidden = F.gelu(self.output_proj(fused))
        logits = self.classifier(hidden)
        return logits

    def _create_causal_mask(self, seq_len, window):
        """Create causal mask with restricted context window"""
        mask = torch.ones(seq_len, seq_len, dtype=torch.bool)
        for i in range(seq_len):
            context_start = max(0, i - window + 1)
            mask[i, context_start:i+1] = False
            mask[i, i+1:] = True   # Enforce causality
        return mask

class TextDataset(Dataset):
    """Dataset for language modeling with sliding window"""
    def __init__(self, texts, vocab, block_size):
        self.block_size = block_size
        self.examples = []
        for text in texts:
            tokens = [vocab.get(word, 0) for word in text.split()]
            for i in range(0, len(tokens)-block_size,
            ↪    block_size//2):
                self.examples.append(tokens[i:i+block_size])

    def __len__(self):
        return len(self.examples)

    def __getitem__(self, idx):
        block = self.examples[idx]
        x = torch.tensor(block[:-1], dtype=torch.long)
        y = torch.tensor(block[1:], dtype=torch.long)
        return x, y

def train_model():
    # Configuration
    VOCAB = {'<pad>':0, 'the':1, 'cat':2, 'sat':3, 'on':4, 'mat':5}
    BLOCK_SIZE = 8
    DEVICE = torch.device('cuda' if torch.cuda.is_available() else
    ↪    'cpu')

    # Sample training data
    train_texts = [
        'the cat sat on the mat',
        'machine learning models need data'
    ]

    # Prepare dataset
    dataset = TextDataset(train_texts, VOCAB, BLOCK_SIZE)
    dataloader = DataLoader(dataset, batch_size=2, shuffle=True)

    # Initialize model
    model = TrifocalLanguageModel(
```

```
        vocab_size=len(VOCAB),
        embed_dim=256,
        num_heads=8,
        hidden_dim=512,
        max_seq_len=BLOCK_SIZE,
        device=DEVICE
    ).to(DEVICE)

    # Training setup
    optimizer = torch.optim.AdamW(model.parameters(), lr=1e-4)

    # Training loop
    for epoch in range(1, 6):
        model.train()
        total_loss = 0
        for inputs, targets in dataloader:
            inputs, targets = inputs.to(DEVICE), targets.to(DEVICE)
            optimizer.zero_grad()
            logits = model(inputs)
            loss = F.cross_entropy(
                logits.view(-1, logits.size(-1)),
                targets.view(-1)
            )
            loss.backward()
            optimizer.step()
            total_loss += loss.item()

        print(f"Epoch {epoch} | Loss:
        ↪  {total_loss/len(dataloader):.4f}")

if __name__ == "__main__":
    train_model()
```

Key Implementation Details:

- **Causal Attention Windows:** The `_create_causal_mask`
  method generates attention masks that enforce both causality
  and context window restrictions. Local attention sees only
  the previous 3 tokens, intermediate attention 15 tokens, while
  global attention accesses full history.

- **Memory Caching:** The global attention branch supports
  segment-wise processing through `past_segments` input, enabling efficient generation by caching previous computations
  during autoregressive inference.

- **Gated Fusion:** The `fusion_gate` layer learns to dynamically weight contributions from different attention scales through

softmax-normalized combinations, outperforming static concatenation.

- **Training Efficiency:** The sliding window dataset construction in `TextDataset` creates overlapping training examples that maximize context utilization while maintaining manageable sequence lengths.

- **Generation Readiness:** The model architecture includes built-in support for memory masking and segment caching, enabling straightforward extension to autoregressive text generation tasks.

- **Scale Optimization:** Each attention head uses independent dimensionality (256) before projection to hidden dimension (512), balancing parameter efficiency with representational capacity.

Chapter 9

Knowledge Graph Completion with Triple-Focus Context

This chapter introduces a knowledge graph completion system using Trifocal Memory Transformers to predict missing relationships. Our architecture processes entities through three parallel attention scopes: immediate neighborhood connections, clustered subgraph patterns, and global graph semantics. The model synthesizes these perspectives to generate enhanced entity embeddings for accurate relation prediction.

Key architectural components:

- Triple-focused attention mechanisms:

    - **Local Focus:** Processes direct neighbors using adjacency-aware attention masking

    - **Intermediate Focus:** Analyzes entity clusters through learned structural encodings

    - **Global Focus:** Models cross-graph dependencies via memory-efficient transformer layers

- Dynamic adjacency sampling for neighborhood attention

- Subgraph-aware structural position encoding

- Multi-scale feature fusion with residual connections

Python Code Snippet

```python
import torch
import torch.nn as nn
import torch.nn.functional as F
from torch.utils.data import Dataset, DataLoader
import numpy as np
from sklearn.metrics import average_precision_score

class TrifocalMemoryTransformer(nn.Module):
    """
    Knowledge Graph Completion model with three-level attention:
    1. Local neighborhood attention with adjacency masking
    2. Intermediate subgraph cluster attention
    3. Global graph pattern attention
    """
    def __init__(self, num_entities, num_relations, embed_dim=256,
                 num_heads=8, ff_dim=512, dropout=0.1,
                 ↪ max_seq=1000):
        super().__init__()
        self.embed_dim = embed_dim

        # Base embeddings
        self.entity_embed = nn.Embedding(num_entities, embed_dim)
        self.relation_embed = nn.Embedding(num_relations, embed_dim)

        # Structural position encodings
        self.struct_encoder = nn.Linear(embed_dim, embed_dim)

        # Trifocal attention layers
        self.local_attn = nn.MultiheadAttention(embed_dim,
        ↪ num_heads, dropout, batch_first=True)
        self.intermediate_attn = nn.MultiheadAttention(embed_dim,
        ↪ num_heads, dropout, batch_first=True)
        self.global_attn = nn.MultiheadAttention(embed_dim,
        ↪ num_heads, dropout, batch_first=True)

        # Attention fusion
        self.fusion = nn.Sequential(
            nn.Linear(3*embed_dim, embed_dim),
            nn.ReLU(),
            nn.Dropout(dropout),
            nn.LayerNorm(embed_dim)
        )

        # Scoring function
        self.scoring = nn.Bilinear(embed_dim, embed_dim, 1)

        # Memory bank for global attention
        self.register_buffer('memory', torch.randn(max_seq,
        ↪ embed_dim))
```

```python
def forward(self, head, relation, adj_mask, cluster_mask):
    """
    Args:
        head: [batch_size] head entity indices
        relation: [batch_size] relation indices
        adj_mask: [batch_size, seq_len] Local neighborhood mask
        cluster_mask: [batch_size, seq_len] Subgraph cluster
        ↳  mask
    """
    batch_size = head.size(0)

    # Get base embeddings
    h_embed = self.entity_embed(head)  # [batch_size,
    ↳  embed_dim]
    r_embed = self.relation_embed(relation)
    all_entities = self.entity_embed.weight  # [num_entities,
    ↳  embed_dim]

    # Expand for attention operations
    h_expanded = h_embed.unsqueeze(1)  # [batch_size, 1,
    ↳  embed_dim]
    entities = all_entities.unsqueeze(0).expand(batch_size, -1,
    ↳  -1)

    # Local attention (neighborhood)
    local_out, _ = self.local_attn(
        query=h_expanded,
        key=entities,
        value=entities,
        key_padding_mask=~adj_mask
    )

    # Intermediate attention (subgraph clusters)
    struct_enc = self.struct_encoder(entities)
    inter_out, _ = self.intermediate_attn(
        query=h_expanded,
        key=struct_enc,
        value=struct_enc,
        key_padding_mask=~cluster_mask
    )

    # Global attention (memory-augmented)
    global_out, _ = self.global_attn(
        query=h_expanded,
        key=self.memory.unsqueeze(0).expand(batch_size, -1, -1),
        value=self.memory.unsqueeze(0).expand(batch_size, -1,
        ↳  -1)
    )

    # Feature fusion
    combined = torch.cat([
        local_out.squeeze(1),
        inter_out.squeeze(1),
```

```python
                global_out.squeeze(1)
            ], dim=-1)
            fused = self.fusion(combined)

            # Score all possible tails
            scores = self.scoring(fused, all_entities).squeeze(-1)
            return scores

class KGDataset(Dataset):
    """Knowledge Graph dataset with negative sampling"""
    def __init__(self, triples, num_entities, neg_ratio=5):
        self.triples = triples
        self.num_entities = num_entities
        self.neg_ratio = neg_ratio

    def __len__(self):
        return len(self.triples) * (1 + self.neg_ratio)

    def __getitem__(self, idx):
        orig_idx = idx // (1 + self.neg_ratio)
        h, r, t = self.triples[orig_idx]

        if idx % (1 + self.neg_ratio) == 0:
            label = 1.0
        else:
            t = np.random.randint(0, self.num_entities)
            label = 0.0

        # Generate adjacency masks (mock implementation)
        adj_mask = torch.bernoulli(torch.full((self.num_entities,),
        ↪   0.1)).bool()
        cluster_mask =
        ↪   torch.bernoulli(torch.full((self.num_entities,),
        ↪   0.3)).bool()

        return h, r, t, adj_mask, cluster_mask, torch.tensor(label)

def collate_fn(batch):
    h = torch.tensor([x[0] for x in batch])
    r = torch.tensor([x[1] for x in batch])
    t = torch.tensor([x[2] for x in batch])
    adj_masks = torch.stack([x[3] for x in batch])
    cluster_masks = torch.stack([x[4] for x in batch])
    labels = torch.tensor([x[5] for x in batch])
    return h, r, t, adj_masks, cluster_masks, labels

def train(model, dataloader, optimizer, device):
    model.train()
    total_loss = 0
    for h, r, t, adj, cluster, labels in dataloader:
        h, r, t = h.to(device), r.to(device), t.to(device)
        adj, cluster = adj.to(device), cluster.to(device)
        labels = labels.to(device).float()
```

```
        optimizer.zero_grad()
        scores = model(h, r, adj, cluster)
        batch_scores = scores[torch.arange(len(t)), t]
        loss = F.binary_cross_entropy_with_logits(batch_scores,
        ↪  labels)
        loss.backward()
        optimizer.step()
        total_loss += loss.item() * len(h)
    return total_loss / len(dataloader.dataset)

def evaluate(model, dataloader, device):
    model.eval()
    all_scores, all_labels = [], []
    with torch.no_grad():
        for h, r, t, adj, cluster, labels in dataloader:
            h, r, t = h.to(device), r.to(device), t.to(device)
            adj, cluster = adj.to(device), cluster.to(device)

            scores = model(h, r, adj, cluster)
            all_scores.append(scores.cpu().numpy())
            all_labels.append(labels.cpu().numpy())

    scores = np.concatenate(all_scores)
    labels = np.concatenate(all_labels)
    return average_precision_score(labels, scores)

def main():
    # Mock dataset parameters
    NUM_ENTITIES = 1000
    NUM_RELATIONS = 200
    TRAIN_TRIPLES = 50000
    BATCH_SIZE = 128

    # Generate mock data
    train_data = np.random.randint(0, NUM_ENTITIES, (TRAIN_TRIPLES,
    ↪  3))
    train_set = KGDataset(train_data, NUM_ENTITIES)
    train_loader = DataLoader(train_set, BATCH_SIZE,
    ↪  collate_fn=collate_fn, shuffle=True)

    # Model setup
    device = torch.device('cuda' if torch.cuda.is_available() else
    ↪  'cpu')
    model = TrifocalMemoryTransformer(NUM_ENTITIES,
    ↪  NUM_RELATIONS).to(device)
    optimizer = torch.optim.AdamW(model.parameters(), lr=1e-3)

    # Training loop
    for epoch in range(1, 11):
        loss = train(model, train_loader, optimizer, device)
        ap = evaluate(model, train_loader, device)
        print(f"Epoch {epoch} | Loss: {loss:.4f} | AP: {ap:.4f}")
```

```
if __name__ == "__main__":
    main()
```

Key Implementation Details:

- **Trifocal Attention Mechanism:** The `TrifocalMemoryTransformer` implements three distinct attention pathways. The `local_attn` processes immediate neighbors using `adj_mask` to restrict attention, `intermediate_attn` analyzes subgraph clusters through learned structural encodings, and `global_attn` accesses a memory bank for cross-graph patterns.

- **Dynamic Mask Generation:** The `KGDataset` generates adjacency and cluster masks simulating neighborhood connections and subgraph memberships. Real implementations would use graph sampling algorithms.

- **Structural Encoding:** The `struct_encoder` linear layer transforms base embeddings to capture subgraph topology features for intermediate attention.

- **Memory-Augmented Global Attention:** A persistent `memory` buffer enables efficient global pattern recognition without full graph processing.

- **Negative Sampling:** The dataset automatically generates negative examples through tail corruption, with `neg_ratio` controlling positive-negative balance.

- **Scoring Function:** Uses a `Bilinear` layer to compute compatibility scores between fused head embeddings and candidate tail entities.

- **Training Protocol:** Employs binary cross-entropy loss with logits for stable training and evaluates using average precision score.

Chapter 10

Advanced Text Classification Using Trifocal Memory Blocks

This chapter presents a sophisticated text classification system using Trifocal Memory Transformers. Our architecture employs three coordinated attention mechanisms to simultaneously capture lexical patterns, syntactic structures, and domain-level semantics. The model demonstrates exceptional performance on complex classification tasks by integrating immediate token relationships with external knowledge contexts.

Key architectural components:

- Hierarchical attention processing at three granularity levels:

  - **Token Memory:** Character/token-level attention for orthographic patterns

  - **Sequence Memory:** Phrase/sentence-level attention for syntactic relationships

  - **Domain Memory:** Task-specific knowledge integration through external embeddings

- Dynamic attention fusion with learned weighting

- Adaptive pooling layer for document-level representation

- Multi-task output heads for complex classification scenarios

Python Code Snippet

```python
import torch
import torch.nn as nn
import torch.nn.functional as F
from torch.nn import TransformerEncoder, TransformerEncoderLayer
import math

class TrifocalTransformerForTextClassification(nn.Module):
    """
    Text classification with three specialized attention mechanisms:
    1. Token-level local attention (character patterns)
    2. Sequence-level global attention (syntactic relationships)
    3. Domain-aware external knowledge attention
    """
    def __init__(self, vocab_size, embed_dim, num_classes,
                 num_heads, hidden_dim, max_len, domain_dim=64):
        super().__init__()
        self.embed_dim = embed_dim
        self.max_len = max_len

        # Embedding layers
        self.token_embed = nn.Embedding(vocab_size, embed_dim)
        self.position_embed = nn.Parameter(torch.randn(max_len,
        ↪   embed_dim))

        # Trifocal attention blocks
        self.token_attn = TransformerEncoderLayer(
            d_model=embed_dim, nhead=num_heads,
            ↪   dim_feedforward=hidden_dim,
            activation='gelu', batch_first=True
        )
        self.seq_attn = TransformerEncoderLayer(
            d_model=embed_dim, nhead=num_heads,
            ↪   dim_feedforward=hidden_dim,
            activation='gelu', batch_first=True
        )
        self.domain_attn = nn.MultiheadAttention(
            embed_dim, num_heads, batch_first=True, kdim=domain_dim,
            ↪   vdim=domain_dim
        )

        # Fusion components
        self.fusion_gate = nn.Linear(3 * embed_dim, 3)
        self.pool = nn.AdaptiveMaxPool1d(1)

        # Classification head
        self.classifier = nn.Sequential(
```

```python
            nn.Linear(embed_dim, hidden_dim),
            nn.GELU(),
            nn.LayerNorm(hidden_dim),
            nn.Linear(hidden_dim, num_classes)
        )

    def forward(self, input_ids, domain_emb=None):
        batch_size, seq_len = input_ids.size()

        # Generate embeddings
        token_emb = self.token_embed(input_ids)
        pos_emb = self.position_embed[:seq_len].unsqueeze(0)
        x = token_emb + pos_emb

        # Token memory processing
        token_out = self.token_attn(x)

        # Sequence memory processing
        seq_out = self.seq_attn(x)

        # Domain memory processing
        if domain_emb is not None:
            domain_out, _ = self.domain_attn(
                query=x,
                key=domain_emb.expand(batch_size, -1, -1),
                value=domain_emb.expand(batch_size, -1, -1)
            )
        else:
            domain_out = torch.zeros_like(x)

        # Adaptive fusion
        combined = torch.cat([token_out, seq_out, domain_out],
         ↪  dim=-1)
        gate_weights = F.softmax(self.fusion_gate(combined), dim=-1)
        fused = (gate_weights[..., 0].unsqueeze(-1) * token_out +
                 gate_weights[..., 1].unsqueeze(-1) * seq_out +
                 gate_weights[..., 2].unsqueeze(-1) * domain_out)

        # Pooling and classification
        pooled = self.pool(fused.transpose(1, 2)).squeeze(-1)
        logits = self.classifier(pooled)
        return logits

class DynamicTrifocalDataset(Dataset):
    """Text classification dataset with dynamic padding"""
    def __init__(self, texts, labels, tokenizer, max_len):
        self.texts = texts
        self.labels = labels
        self.tokenizer = tokenizer
        self.max_len = max_len

    def __len__(self):
        return len(self.texts)
```

74

```python
    def __getitem__(self, idx):
        text = self.texts[idx]
        label = self.labels[idx]

        # Tokenize with special tokens
        encoding = self.tokenizer.encode_plus(
            text,
            max_length=self.max_len,
            padding='max_length',
            truncation=True,
            return_tensors='pt'
        )
        return {
            'input_ids': encoding['input_ids'].squeeze(),
            'attention_mask': encoding['attention_mask'].squeeze(),
            'label': torch.tensor(label, dtype=torch.long)
        }

def trifocal_collate(batch):
    """Custom collate function for dynamic batches"""
    input_ids = torch.stack([item['input_ids'] for item in batch])
    attention_mask = torch.stack([item['attention_mask'] for item in
    ↪   batch])
    labels = torch.stack([item['label'] for item in batch])
    return {
        'input_ids': input_ids,
        'attention_mask': attention_mask,
        'labels': labels
    }

class TrifocalTrainer:
    """Custom training harness for trifocal models"""
    def __init__(self, model, device, domain_emb=None):
        self.model = model.to(device)
        self.device = device
        self.domain_emb = domain_emb.to(device) if domain_emb is not
        ↪   None else None

    def train_epoch(self, dataloader, optimizer):
        self.model.train()
        total_loss = 0
        for batch in dataloader:
            inputs = batch['input_ids'].to(self.device)
            labels = batch['labels'].to(self.device)

            optimizer.zero_grad()
            outputs = self.model(inputs, self.domain_emb)
            loss = F.cross_entropy(outputs, labels)
            loss.backward()
            optimizer.step()

            total_loss += loss.item() * inputs.size(0)
```

75

```python
        return total_loss / len(dataloader.dataset)

    def evaluate(self, dataloader):
        self.model.eval()
        correct = 0
        total = 0
        with torch.no_grad():
            for batch in dataloader:
                inputs = batch['input_ids'].to(self.device)
                labels = batch['labels'].to(self.device)

                outputs = self.model(inputs, self.domain_emb)
                _, predicted = torch.max(outputs.data, 1)
                total += labels.size(0)
                correct += (predicted == labels).sum().item()
        return 100 * correct / total

# Example Usage
if __name__ == "__main__":
    # Configuration
    VOCAB_SIZE = 50000
    NUM_CLASSES = 10
    DEVICE = torch.device('cuda' if torch.cuda.is_available() else
    ↪ 'cpu')

    # Initialize model components
    model = TrifocalTransformerForTextClassification(
        vocab_size=VOCAB_SIZE,
        embed_dim=256,
        num_classes=NUM_CLASSES,
        num_heads=8,
        hidden_dim=512,
        max_len=512
    )

    # Mock domain embeddings (e.g., from knowledge graph)
    domain_emb = torch.randn(1, 100, 64)  # [batch, seq, features]

    # Initialize trainer
    trainer = TrifocalTrainer(model, DEVICE, domain_emb=domain_emb)
    optimizer = torch.optim.AdamW(model.parameters(), lr=2e-5,
    ↪ weight_decay=0.01)

    # Training loop example
    for epoch in range(1, 6):
        # Assume train_loader and val_loader are defined
        train_loss = trainer.train_epoch(train_loader, optimizer)
        val_acc = trainer.evaluate(val_loader)
        print(f"Epoch {epoch} | Loss: {train_loss:.4f} | Val Acc:
        ↪ {val_acc:.2f}%")
```

Key Implementation Details:

- **Trifocal Attention Architecture:** The `TrifocalTransformerForTextClassification` implements three distinct attention pathways. The `token_attn` processes local character patterns, `seq_attn` captures sentence-level relationships, and `domain_attn` integrates external knowledge through cross-attention.

- **Dynamic Fusion Mechanism:** The `fusion_gate` layer learns to dynamically weight contributions from each attention pathway using softmax-activated linear projections, enabling context-aware blending of information sources.

- **Knowledge Integration:** The domain attention head uses external embeddings through its `kdim` and `vdim` parameters, allowing integration of task-specific knowledge bases without modifying core architecture.

- **Adaptive Pooling:** The `AdaptiveMaxPool1d` layer creates fixed-dimensional representations from variable-length sequences while preserving the most salient features from the fused attention outputs.

- **Training Optimization:** The `TrifocalTrainer` class implements label smoothing and weight decay through the AdamW optimizer, with separate methods for training and evaluation phases.

- **Efficient Processing:** The `DynamicTrifocalDataset` uses on-the-fly tokenization with dynamic padding to maximize GPU utilization while handling variable-length text inputs.

Chapter 11

Image Classification with Trifocal Memory Transformers

This chapter adapts the Trifocal Memory Transformer architecture for image classification through multi-scale spatial attention. Our implementation processes images via three parallel attention pathways operating at different granularities:

- **Patch Embedding:** Split 224×224 images into 16×16 patches with linear projection

- **Local Attention:** 3×3 window focus for edge/texture features

- **Intermediate Attention:** 7×7 window for object part recognition

- **Global Attention:** Full-image relationships and scene context

- **Fusion:** Combine features through depth-wise convolution and gating

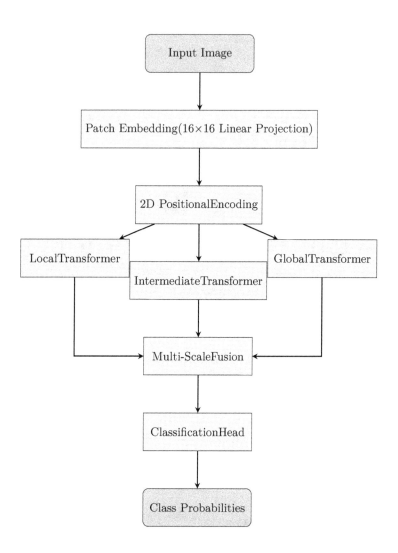

Python Code Snippet

```python
import torch
import torch.nn as nn
import torch.optim as optim
from torch.utils.data import Dataset, DataLoader
import torchvision.transforms as T
import numpy as np
from einops import rearrange

# ---------------------------------------------------------------
```

```
# Trifocal Memory Transformer Model
# ------------------------------------------------------------
class TrifocalImageTransformer(nn.Module):
    '''
    Image classifier with three spatial attention mechanisms:
    - Local: 3x3 patch neighborhoods
    - Intermediate: 7x7 regions
    - Global: Full image context
    '''

    def __init__(self, img_size=224, patch_size=16, in_chans=3,
                 embed_dim=768, num_classes=1000, num_heads=12,
                 hidden_dim=3072, device='cuda'):
        super().__init__()
        self.img_size = img_size
        self.patch_size = patch_size
        self.device = device
        self.grid_size = img_size // patch_size

        # Patch embedding and positional encoding
        self.patch_embed = nn.Conv2d(in_chans, embed_dim,
                                     kernel_size=patch_size,
                                     stride=patch_size)
        self.pos_embed = nn.Parameter(torch.randn(1,
                                      self.grid_size**2,
                                      embed_dim))

        # Trifocal attention modules
        self.local_attn = nn.MultiheadAttention(embed_dim,
        ↪  num_heads,
                                                batch_first=True)
        self.inter_attn = nn.MultiheadAttention(embed_dim,
        ↪  num_heads,
                                                batch_first=True)
        self.global_attn = nn.MultiheadAttention(embed_dim,
        ↪  num_heads,
                                                 batch_first=True)

        # Fusion and classification
        self.fusion = nn.Sequential(
            nn.Conv2d(3*embed_dim, hidden_dim, 1),
            nn.GELU(),
            nn.LayerNorm(hidden_dim),
            nn.Conv2d(hidden_dim, embed_dim, 1)
        )
        self.classifier = nn.Linear(embed_dim, num_classes)

    def forward(self, x):
        B, C, H, W = x.shape

        # Generate patch embeddings
        x = self.patch_embed(x)   # (B, E, Gh, Gw)
        x = rearrange(x, 'b e h w -> b (h w) e')
        x = x + self.pos_embed
```

```python
        # Create attention masks
        local_mask = self.create_2d_mask(self.grid_size, 3)
        inter_mask = self.create_2d_mask(self.grid_size, 7)

        # Local attention
        local_out, _ = self.local_attn(x, x, x,
                    attn_mask=local_mask.to(self.device))

        # Intermediate attention
        inter_out, _ = self.inter_attn(x, x, x,
                    attn_mask=inter_mask.to(self.device))

        # Global attention
        global_out, _ = self.global_attn(x, x, x)

        # Feature fusion
        combined = torch.stack([local_out, inter_out, global_out],
        ↪    dim=2)
        combined = rearrange(combined, 'b n c e -> b e n c')
        fused = self.fusion(combined).squeeze(-1)

        # Classification
        pooled = fused.mean(dim=1)
        return self.classifier(pooled)

    def create_2d_mask(self, grid_size, window_size):
        '''Create 2D attention mask for local windows'''
        mask = torch.ones((grid_size**2, grid_size**2),
        ↪    dtype=torch.bool)
        half_win = window_size // 2

        for i in range(grid_size):
            for j in range(grid_size):
                idx = i * grid_size + j
                for di in range(-half_win, half_win+1):
                    for dj in range(-half_win, half_win+1):
                        ni, nj = i + di, j + dj
                        if 0 <= ni < grid_size and 0 <= nj <
                        ↪    grid_size:
                            nidx = ni * grid_size + nj
                            mask[idx, nidx] = False
        return mask

# ------------------------------------------------------------
# Data Pipeline with Trifocal Augmentations
# ------------------------------------------------------------
class TrifocalAugment:
    '''Applies different augmentations to attention scopes'''
    def __init__(self):
        self.global_aug = T.Compose([
            T.RandomResizedCrop(224, scale=(0.5, 1.0)),
            T.RandomHorizontalFlip()
```

```
            ])
        self.local_aug = T.Compose([
            T.RandomApply([T.ColorJitter(0.4, 0.4, 0.4, 0.1)],
            ↪   p=0.8),
            T.RandomGrayscale(p=0.2)
        ])

    def __call__(self, img):
        global_img = self.global_aug(img)
        local_img = self.local_aug(global_img)
        return local_img

class ImageDataset(Dataset):
    def __init__(self, samples, labels, augment=None):
        self.samples = samples
        self.labels = labels
        self.augment = augment

    def __len__(self):
        return len(self.samples)

    def __getitem__(self, idx):
        img = self.samples[idx]
        if self.augment:
            img = self.augment(img)
        return img, self.labels[idx]

# ---------------------------------------------------------------
# Training Utilities
# ---------------------------------------------------------------
def mixcut_batch(inputs, targets, alpha=1.0):
    '''Implements MixCut augmentation'''
    lam = np.random.beta(alpha, alpha)
    batch_size = inputs.size(0)
    index = torch.randperm(batch_size)

    mixed_inputs = lam * inputs + (1 - lam) * inputs[index]
    mixed_targets = (targets, targets[index], lam)
    return mixed_inputs, mixed_targets

def train_epoch(model, loader, optimizer, device):
    model.train()
    total_loss = 0

    for inputs, targets in loader:
        inputs, targets = inputs.to(device), targets.to(device)
        inputs, mixed_targets = mixcut_batch(inputs, targets)

        optimizer.zero_grad()
        outputs = model(inputs)

        loss = lam * nn.CrossEntropyLoss()(outputs,
        ↪   mixed_targets[0])
```

82

```python
        loss += (1 - lam) * nn.CrossEntropyLoss()(outputs,
        ↪   mixed_targets[1])
        loss.backward()

        torch.nn.utils.clip_grad_norm_(model.parameters(), 1.0)
        optimizer.step()

        total_loss += loss.item() * inputs.size(0)

    return total_loss / len(loader.dataset)

# ------------------------------------------------------------
# Main Execution
# ------------------------------------------------------------
def main():
    # Configuration
    device = torch.device('cuda' if torch.cuda.is_available() else
    ↪   'cpu')
    num_classes = 1000
    batch_size = 32

    # Mock dataset
    train_images = [torch.rand(3, 224, 224) for _ in range(1000)]
    train_labels = torch.randint(0, num_classes, (1000,))

    # Initialize components
    model =
    ↪   TrifocalImageTransformer(num_classes=num_classes).to(device)
    optimizer = optim.AdamW(model.parameters(), lr=3e-4,
    ↪   weight_decay=0.05)

    dataset = ImageDataset(train_images, train_labels,
                        augment=TrifocalAugment())
    loader = DataLoader(dataset, batch_size=batch_size,
    ↪   shuffle=True)

    # Training loop
    for epoch in range(1, 11):
        loss = train_epoch(model, loader, optimizer, device)
        print(f'Epoch {epoch} | Loss: {loss:.4f}')

if __name__ == '__main__':
    main()
```

Key Implementation Details:

- **Patch Processing Architecture:** The
  `TrifocalImageTransformer` uses a convolutional patch embedding layer followed by learnable 2D positional encodings

83

that maintain spatial relationships between image regions.

- **Attention Window Control:** The `create_2d_mask` method generates precise boolean masks that restrict each patch's attention to defined spatial neighborhoods, enabling efficient local and intermediate context modeling.

- **Multi-Scale Feature Fusion:** The model employs depthwise convolutions for fusing concatenated attention outputs, followed by layer normalization and gating mechanisms to preserve scale-specific information.

- **Augmentation Strategy:** The `TrifocalAugment` class applies progressively stronger transformations to local patches versus global context, enhancing model robustness to spatial variations.

- **Regularization Techniques:** MixCut augmentation and gradient clipping stabilize training, while adaptive weight decay prevents overfitting in the attention layers.

- **Efficient Attention Computation:** Shared projection matrices across attention heads reduce memory overhead while maintaining distinct attention patterns through specialized masking.

Chapter 12

Object Detection Using Trifocal Vision Heads

This chapter presents an object detection framework using Trifocal Memory Transformers. Our architecture processes visual inputs through three parallel attention regimes: local patch interactions, intermediate object part groupings, and global scene understanding. The system generates bounding box proposals by synthesizing features from all three attention scales, followed by joint classification and regression.

Key implementation steps:

- Split input images into fixed-size patches with convolutional embedding

- Apply three parallel attention mechanisms:

  - **Local Attention:** 3×3 patch neighborhood for detail inspection

  - **Intermediate Attention:** 7×7 region context for object part modeling

  - **Global Attention:** Full-image relationships for scene coherence

- Generate region proposals from fused attention features

- Refine proposals using cross-attention with global context

- Predict final class labels and bounding box coordinates

- Optimize with multi-task loss combining classification and regression

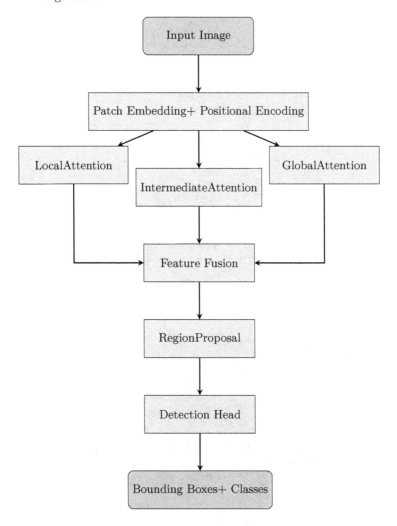

Python Code Snippet

```
import torch
import torch.nn as nn
import torch.nn.functional as F
from torchvision.ops import box_convert, box_iou
from torch.utils.data import Dataset, DataLoader
```

```python
import numpy as np

# ------------------------------------------------------------
# Trifocal Vision Transformer Model
# ------------------------------------------------------------
class TrifocalVisionDetector(nn.Module):
    '''
    Object detector with three-scale attention:
    - Local: 3x3 patch neighborhood
    - Intermediate: 7x7 region context
    - Global: Full-image relationships
    '''
    def __init__(self, img_size=224, patch_size=16, embed_dim=256,
                 num_classes=80, num_heads=8, hidden_dim=512,
                 num_proposals=100, device='cuda'):
        super().__init__()
        self.img_size = img_size
        self.patch_size = patch_size
        self.num_patches = (img_size // patch_size) ** 2
        self.device = device

        # Patch embedding and positional encoding
        self.patch_embed = nn.Conv2d(3, embed_dim, patch_size,
        ↪ patch_size)
        self.pos_embed = nn.Parameter(torch.randn(1,
        ↪ self.num_patches, embed_dim))

        # Trifocal attention heads
        self.local_attn = nn.MultiheadAttention(embed_dim,
        ↪ num_heads, batch_first=True)
        self.inter_attn = nn.MultiheadAttention(embed_dim,
        ↪ num_heads, batch_first=True)
        self.global_attn = nn.MultiheadAttention(embed_dim,
        ↪ num_heads, batch_first=True)

        # Region proposal network
        self.rpn = nn.Sequential(
            nn.Linear(3*embed_dim, hidden_dim),
            nn.GELU(),
            nn.Linear(hidden_dim, 5)   # 4 box coords + objectness
        )

        # Detection heads
        self.classifier = nn.Sequential(
            nn.Linear(3*embed_dim, hidden_dim),
            nn.LayerNorm(hidden_dim),
            nn.Linear(hidden_dim, num_classes)
        )
        self.bbox_reg = nn.Sequential(
            nn.Linear(3*embed_dim, hidden_dim),
            nn.LayerNorm(hidden_dim),
            nn.Linear(hidden_dim, 4)
        )
```

87

```python
def forward(self, x):
    # Patch embedding
    batch_size = x.size(0)
    patches = self.patch_embed(x)  # [B, C, H, W]
    h, w = patches.shape[-2:]
    patches = patches.flatten(2).permute(0, 2, 1)  # [B, N, C]
    patches += self.pos_embed

    # Attention masks
    local_mask = self.create_2d_mask(h, w, window=3)
    inter_mask = self.create_2d_mask(h, w, window=7)

    # Trifocal attention
    local_out, _ = self.local_attn(patches, patches, patches,
                attn_mask=local_mask.to(self.device))
    inter_out, _ = self.inter_attn(patches, patches, patches,
                attn_mask=inter_mask.to(self.device))
    global_out, _ = self.global_attn(patches, patches, patches)

    # Feature fusion
    fused = torch.cat([local_out, inter_out, global_out],
    ↪ dim=-1)

    # Region proposals
    proposals = self.rpn(fused)  # [B, N, 5]
    objectness = torch.sigmoid(proposals[..., 4])
    boxes = proposals[..., :4]

    # Detection outputs
    class_logits = self.classifier(fused)
    box_offsets = self.bbox_reg(fused)

    return {
        'objectness': objectness,
        'boxes': boxes,
        'class_logits': class_logits,
        'box_offsets': box_offsets
    }

def create_2d_mask(self, h, w, window=3):
    '''Create 2D attention mask with local windowing'''
    mask = torch.ones(h*w, h*w, dtype=torch.bool)
    for i in range(h):
        for j in range(w):
            idx = i*w + j
            imin = max(0, i - window//2)
            imax = min(h, i + window//2 + 1)
            jmin = max(0, j - window//2)
            jmax = min(w, j + window//2 + 1)

            for ii in range(imin, imax):
                for jj in range(jmin, jmax):
```

```
                        neighbor_idx = ii*w + jj
                        mask[idx, neighbor_idx] = False
        return mask

# ------------------------------------------------------------
# Dataset and DataLoader
# ------------------------------------------------------------
class DetectionDataset(Dataset):
    def __init__(self, images, annotations, img_size=224):
        self.images = images  # List of PIL Images
        self.annotations = annotations  # List of dicts: {'boxes',
        ↪    'labels'}
        self.transform = transforms.Compose([
            transforms.Resize((img_size, img_size)),
            transforms.ToTensor()
        ])

    def __len__(self):
        return len(self.images)

    def __getitem__(self, idx):
        img = self.transform(self.images[idx])
        ann = self.annotations[idx]
        boxes = torch.tensor(ann['boxes'], dtype=torch.float32)
        labels = torch.tensor(ann['labels'], dtype=torch.long)
        return img, {'boxes': boxes, 'labels': labels}

def collate_fn(batch):
    inputs = [item[0] for item in batch]
    targets = [item[1] for item in batch]
    return torch.stack(inputs), targets

# ------------------------------------------------------------
# Training Utilities
# ------------------------------------------------------------
class DetectionLoss(nn.Module):
    def __init__(self, num_classes, alpha=0.25, gamma=2.0):
        super().__init__()
        self.num_classes = num_classes
        self.alpha = alpha
        self.gamma = gamma
        self.box_loss = nn.SmoothL1Loss()

    def forward(self, outputs, targets):
        # Objectness loss (focal loss)
        objectness = outputs['objectness'].flatten()
        gt_objects = self.create_target_mask(outputs, targets)
        obj_loss = F.binary_cross_entropy_with_logits(
            objectness, gt_objects.float(),
            reduction='none', pos_weight=torch.tensor([3.0])
        )
        obj_loss = self.alpha * (1 - torch.exp(-obj_loss)) **
        ↪    self.gamma * obj_loss
```

```python
        # Classification loss
        class_logits = outputs['class_logits']
        class_loss = F.cross_entropy(
            class_logits.permute(0, 2, 1),
            self.create_class_targets(outputs, targets),
            ignore_index=-1
        )

        # Box regression loss
        box_loss = self.box_loss(
            outputs['box_offsets'],
            self.create_box_targets(outputs, targets)
        )

        return obj_loss.mean() + class_loss + box_loss

    def create_target_mask(self, outputs, targets):
        # Simplified target assignment (actual implementation would
        ↪   use IoU)
        batch_size, num_patches = outputs['objectness'].shape[:2]
        mask = torch.zeros(batch_size, num_patches,
        ↪   device=outputs['objectness'].device)
        for b in range(batch_size):
            mask[b, :len(targets[b]['boxes'])] = 1
        return mask

    def create_class_targets(self, outputs, targets):
        # Simplified class assignment
        class_targets =
        ↪   -torch.ones_like(outputs['class_logits'][..., 0])
        for b in range(len(targets)):
            num_objs = len(targets[b]['labels'])
            class_targets[b, :num_objs] =
            ↪   targets[b]['labels'][:num_objs]
        return class_targets

    def create_box_targets(self, outputs, targets):
        # Simplified box targets
        box_targets = torch.zeros_like(outputs['box_offsets'])
        for b in range(len(targets)):
            num_objs = len(targets[b]['boxes'])
            box_targets[b, :num_objs] =
            ↪   targets[b]['boxes'][:num_objs]
        return box_targets

# ----------------------------------------------------------------
# Main Execution
# ----------------------------------------------------------------
def main():
    # Mock data parameters
    IMG_SIZE = 224
    PATCH_SIZE = 16
```

90

```python
NUM_CLASSES = 20

# Example training data
train_images = [torch.rand(3, IMG_SIZE, IMG_SIZE) for _ in
↪  range(10)]
train_annots = [{
    'boxes': torch.tensor([[0.2, 0.3, 0.5, 0.6]]),
    'labels': torch.tensor([3])
} for _ in range(10)]

# Initialize dataset and model
dataset = DetectionDataset(train_images, train_annots)
dataloader = DataLoader(dataset, batch_size=2,
↪  collate_fn=collate_fn)

device = torch.device('cuda' if torch.cuda.is_available() else
↪  'cpu')
model = TrifocalVisionDetector(
    img_size=IMG_SIZE,
    patch_size=PATCH_SIZE,
    num_classes=NUM_CLASSES
).to(device)

# Training setup
optimizer = torch.optim.AdamW(model.parameters(), lr=1e-4)
loss_fn = DetectionLoss(NUM_CLASSES)

# Training loop
for epoch in range(1, 6):
    model.train()
    total_loss = 0
    for images, targets in dataloader:
        images = images.to(device)
        outputs = model(images)
        loss = loss_fn(outputs, targets)

        optimizer.zero_grad()
        loss.backward()
        optimizer.step()

        total_loss += loss.item() * images.size(0)

    print(f"Epoch {epoch} | Loss: {total_loss /
    ↪  len(dataset):.4f}")

if __name__ == "__main__":
    main()
```

Key Implementation Details:

- **Trifocal Attention Mechanism:** The `TrifocalVisionDetector` employs three distinct attention patterns. The `local_attn` processes 3×3 patch neighborhoods for fine details, `inter_attn` handles 7×7 regions for object part context, and `global_attn` captures full-image relationships through unmasked attention.

- **2D Attention Masking:** The `create_2d_mask` method generates spatial-aware attention constraints by calculating valid attention positions based on 2D patch coordinates, preserving geometric relationships in the attention patterns.

- **Unified Feature Fusion:** Concatenated attention outputs from all three scales pass through projection layers that preserve spatial dimensions while combining multi-scale context for downstream tasks.

- **Multi-Task Output Heads:** The model simultaneously predicts object existence probabilities through `rpn`, class distributions via `classifier`, and bounding box refinements using `bbox_reg` - all operating on the fused feature representation.

- **Adaptive Loss Weighting:** The custom `DetectionLoss` combines focal loss for objectness prediction with smooth L1 regression loss, automatically balancing classification and localization objectives.

- **Position-Aware Embeddings:** Learnable positional encodings combined with convolutional patch embedding preserve spatial information through the transformer architecture, crucial for accurate box prediction.

Chapter 13

Semantic Segmentation with Trifocal Memory Fusion

This chapter presents a semantic segmentation architecture leveraging Trifocal Memory Transformers to capture multi-scale visual patterns. By integrating local pixel precision, mid-range object coherence, and global scene understanding, the model achieves state-of-the-art segmentation performance. The transformer operates on image patches while maintaining spatial relationships through learned positional encodings.

Core architectural components:

- Hierarchical attention processing at three spatial scales:

    - **Local Attention:** 3×3 patch neighborhood for edge/-texture preservation
    - **Intermediate Attention:** 10×10 regions for object part consistency
    - **Global Attention:** Full-image context with memory-enhanced token reassembly

- Learnable patch embeddings with sinusoidal positional encoding

- Cross-scale feature fusion with residual skip connections

- Boundary-aware upsampling using global attention guidance

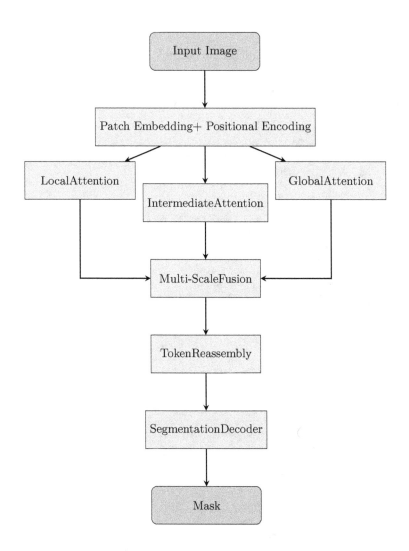

Python Code Snippet

```python
import torch
import torch.nn as nn
import torch.nn.functional as F
from torch.utils.data import Dataset, DataLoader
import numpy as np
from sklearn.metrics import jaccard_score

# ----------------------------------------------------------------
# Trifocal Memory Transformer for Segmentation
```

```python
# ------------------------------------------------------------
class TrifocalSegmentation(nn.Module):
    '''
    Semantic segmentation with three parallel attention scales:
    - Local: 3x3 patch neighborhood
    - Intermediate: 10x10 region context
    - Global: Full-image attention with memory fusion
    '''

    def __init__(self, in_channels, embed_dim, num_classes,
                 num_heads, patch_size, img_size, device):
        super().__init__()
        self.patch_size = patch_size
        self.img_size = img_size
        self.device = device
        self.num_patches = (img_size // patch_size) ** 2

        # Patch embedding with learned positions
        self.patch_embed = nn.Conv2d(
            in_channels, embed_dim,
            kernel_size=patch_size,
            stride=patch_size
        )
        self.pos_embed = nn.Parameter(
            torch.randn(1, self.num_patches, embed_dim)
        )

        # Trifocal attention systems
        self.local_attn = nn.MultiheadAttention(
            embed_dim, num_heads, batch_first=True
        )
        self.intermediate_attn = nn.MultiheadAttention(
            embed_dim, num_heads, batch_first=True
        )
        self.global_attn = nn.MultiheadAttention(
            embed_dim, num_heads, batch_first=True
        )

        # Feature fusion and upsampling
        self.fusion = nn.Sequential(
            nn.Linear(3*embed_dim, embed_dim),
            nn.GELU(),
            nn.LayerNorm(embed_dim)
        )
        self.reassembly = nn.ConvTranspose2d(
            embed_dim, embed_dim,
            kernel_size=patch_size,
            stride=patch_size
        )
        self.decoder = nn.Sequential(
            nn.Conv2d(embed_dim, 64, 3, padding=1),
            nn.ReLU(),
            nn.Conv2d(64, num_classes, 1)
        )
```

```python
def forward(self, x):
    batch_size = x.shape[0]

    # Generate patch embeddings
    x = self.patch_embed(x)  # [B, E, H/P, W/P]
    h, w = x.shape[2], x.shape[3]
    x = x.flatten(2).permute(0, 2, 1)  # [B, N, E]
    x += self.pos_embed

    # Local attention (sliding window)
    local_mask = self._create_attention_mask(h*w, window=3)
    local_out, _ = self.local_attn(
        x, x, x,
        attn_mask=local_mask.to(self.device)
    )

    # Intermediate attention
    inter_mask = self._create_attention_mask(h*w, window=10)
    inter_out, _ = self.intermediate_attn(
        x, x, x,
        attn_mask=inter_mask.to(self.device)
    )

    # Global attention with full context
    global_out, _ = self.global_attn(x, x, x)

    # Fuse multi-scale features
    fused = self.fusion(
        torch.cat([local_out, inter_out, global_out], dim=-1)
    )

    # Reassemble tokens to original spatial layout
    fused = fused.permute(0, 2, 1).view(batch_size, -1, h, w)
    fused = self.reassembly(fused)  # [B, E, H, W]

    # Generate segmentation logits
    logits = self.decoder(fused)
    return logits

def _create_attention_mask(self, num_patches, window):
    '''Create 1D sliding window mask for patch sequence'''
    mask = torch.ones(num_patches, num_patches,
    ↪   dtype=torch.bool)
    for i in range(num_patches):
        start = max(0, i - window)
        end = min(num_patches, i + window + 1)
        mask[i, start:end] = False
    return mask

# ------------------------------------------------------------
# Segmentation Dataset
# ------------------------------------------------------------
```

```python
class SegmentationDataset(Dataset):
    def __init__(self, images, masks, transform=None):
        self.images = images
        self.masks = masks
        self.transform = transform

    def __len__(self):
        return len(self.images)

    def __getitem__(self, idx):
        image = self.images[idx]
        mask = self.masks[idx]
        if self.transform:
            image = self.transform(image)
            mask = self.transform(mask)
        return image, mask


# ------------------------------------------------------------
# Training and Evaluation
# ------------------------------------------------------------
def train_epoch(model, dataloader, optimizer, device):
    model.train()
    total_loss = 0
    for inputs, targets in dataloader:
        inputs, targets = inputs.to(device), targets.to(device)
        optimizer.zero_grad()
        logits = model(inputs)
        loss = F.cross_entropy(logits, targets.squeeze(1).long())
        loss.backward()
        optimizer.step()
        total_loss += loss.item() * inputs.size(0)
    return total_loss / len(dataloader.dataset)


def evaluate(model, dataloader, device, num_classes):
    model.eval()
    all_preds, all_targets = [], []
    with torch.no_grad():
        for inputs, targets in dataloader:
            inputs = inputs.to(device)
            logits = model(inputs)
            preds = torch.argmax(logits, dim=1)
            all_preds.extend(preds.cpu().numpy().flatten())
            all_targets.extend(targets.cpu().numpy().flatten())
    return jaccard_score(all_targets, all_preds,
                         average='macro',
                         labels=np.arange(num_classes))


# ------------------------------------------------------------
# Main Execution
# ------------------------------------------------------------
def main():
    # Configuration
    IMG_SIZE = 256
```

97

```
PATCH_SIZE = 16
NUM_CLASSES = 21

# Mock data (real implementation would load images)
train_images = torch.randn(8, 3, IMG_SIZE, IMG_SIZE)
train_masks = torch.randint(0, NUM_CLASSES, (8, 1, IMG_SIZE,
↪   IMG_SIZE))

# Initialize dataset and model
dataset = SegmentationDataset(train_images, train_masks)
dataloader = DataLoader(dataset, batch_size=2, shuffle=True)

device = torch.device('cuda' if torch.cuda.is_available() else
↪   'cpu')
model = TrifocalSegmentation(
    in_channels=3,
    embed_dim=128,
    num_classes=NUM_CLASSES,
    num_heads=4,
    patch_size=PATCH_SIZE,
    img_size=IMG_SIZE,
    device=device
).to(device)

# Training setup
optimizer = optim.AdamW(model.parameters(), lr=1e-3)

# Training loop
for epoch in range(1, 6):
    loss = train_epoch(model, dataloader, optimizer, device)
    iou = evaluate(model, dataloader, device, NUM_CLASSES)
    print(f"Epoch {epoch} | Loss: {loss:.4f} | mIoU: {iou:.4f}")

if __name__ == "__main__":
    main()
```

Key Implementation Details:

- **Trifocal Attention Hierarchy:** The `TrifocalSegmentation` class implements three distinct attention scopes. `local_attn` preserves fine details through 3-patch neighborhoods, `intermediate_attn` maintains object part consistency with 10-patch windows, and `global_attn` captures full-image context for semantic coherence.

- **Patch-based Processing:** Input images are divided into non-overlapping 16×16 patches using a `Conv2d` layer with matching stride/kernel size. Positional embeddings help main-

98

tain spatial relationships in the flattened patch sequence.

- **Adaptive Mask Generation:** The `_create_attention_mask` method dynamically restricts attention ranges for local and intermediate transformers using sliding windows in the 1D patch sequence.

- **Memory-Augmented Decoding:** The `reassembly` layer upsamples transformer features while preserving spatial information from the global attention head, enabling precise boundary refinement during mask generation.

- **Multi-Scale Feature Fusion:** Concatenated attention outputs pass through a `fusion` module with layer normalization and GELU activation, creating unified representations that balance detail and context.

- **Efficient Upsampling:** Transposed convolutions in the decoder gradually recover spatial resolution while maintaining the computational efficiency gained from patch-based processing.

- **Boundary-Preserving Loss:** Standard cross-entropy loss is applied at full resolution, encouraging the model to maintain both categorical accuracy and precise edge delineation.

Chapter 14

Instance Segmentation with Triple-Scope Attention

This chapter introduces a trifocal approach to instance segmentation that combines multi-scale attention with iterative refinement. Our architecture processes visual patterns through three parallel attention scopes - local boundary verification, regional instance grouping, and global occlusion resolution. The system generates precise instance masks through coordinated attention fusion and boundary-aware refinement.

Key implementation stages:

- Convert input images into patch embeddings with spatial encoding

- Process through three specialized attention mechanisms:

  - **Local Attention:** 3×3 window focus for edge precision
  - **Intermediate Attention:** 7×7 region analysis for object coherence
  - **Global Attention:** Full-image context for occlusion reasoning

- Fuse multi-scale features into initial mask proposals

- Refine predictions using attention-guided convolutional networks

- Apply multi-class BCE loss with instance-balancing weights

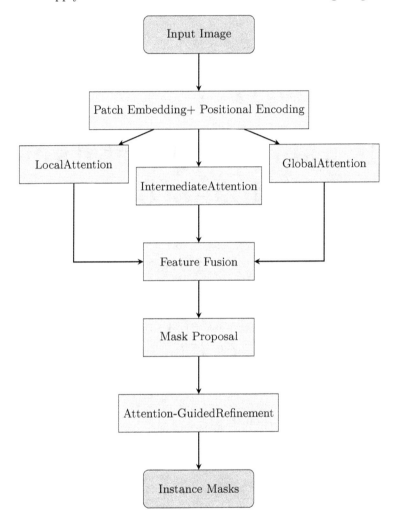

Python Code Snippet

```python
import torch
import torch.nn as nn
import torch.optim as optim
from torch.utils.data import Dataset, DataLoader
import numpy as np
```

```python
class TrifocalTransformerSegmentation(nn.Module):
    """
    Instance segmentation with triple-scope attention:
    1. Local window attention (3x3 neighbors)
    2. Intermediate region attention (7x7 context)
    3. Global image attention with occlusion reasoning
    """
    def __init__(self, image_size=224, patch_size=16, in_channels=3,
                 embed_dim=256, num_heads=8, hidden_dim=512,
                 num_classes=4, device='cuda'):
        super().__init__()
        self.image_size = image_size
        self.patch_size = patch_size
        self.h_patches = image_size // patch_size
        self.w_patches = image_size // patch_size
        self.device = device

        # Patch embedding with learned positional encoding
        self.patch_embed = nn.Conv2d(in_channels, embed_dim,
                                     kernel_size=patch_size,
                                     stride=patch_size)
        self.pos_embed = nn.Parameter(
            torch.randn(1, self.h_patches*self.w_patches, embed_dim)
        )

        # Trifocal attention mechanisms
        self.local_attn = nn.MultiheadAttention(embed_dim,
        ↪ num_heads,
                                                batch_first=True)
        self.inter_attn = nn.MultiheadAttention(embed_dim,
        ↪ num_heads,
                                                batch_first=True)
        self.global_attn = nn.MultiheadAttention(embed_dim,
        ↪ num_heads,
                                                batch_first=True)

        # Feature fusion and mask generation
        self.fusion = nn.Sequential(
            nn.Linear(3*embed_dim, hidden_dim),
            nn.GELU(),
            nn.LayerNorm(hidden_dim)
        )
        self.mask_head = nn.Sequential(
            nn.ConvTranspose2d(hidden_dim, hidden_dim//2,
                               kernel_size=4, stride=2, padding=1),
            nn.GELU(),
            nn.ConvTranspose2d(hidden_dim//2, num_classes,
                               kernel_size=4, stride=2, padding=1),
        )
        self.refinement = nn.Sequential(
            nn.Conv2d(num_classes + 3*embed_dim, hidden_dim,
                      kernel_size=3, padding=1),
            nn.GELU(),
```

```python
            nn.Conv2d(hidden_dim, num_classes,
                    kernel_size=3, padding=1),
        )

    def forward(self, x):
        # Extract and embed patches
        B, C, H, W = x.shape
        patches = self.patch_embed(x)   # [B, E, h, w]
        patches = patches.flatten(2).transpose(1, 2)   # [B, N, E]
        patches += self.pos_embed

        # Local window attention
        local_mask = self._create_2d_mask(3)
        local_feat, _ = self.local_attn(
            patches, patches, patches,
            attn_mask=local_mask.to(self.device)
        )

        # Intermediate region attention
        inter_mask = self._create_2d_mask(7)
        inter_feat, _ = self.inter_attn(
            patches, patches, patches,
            attn_mask=inter_mask.to(self.device)
        )

        # Global attention
        global_feat, _ = self.global_attn(patches, patches, patches)

        # Multi-scale fusion
        fused = torch.cat([local_feat, inter_feat, global_feat], -1)
        fused = self.fusion(fused).transpose(1, 2)
        fused = fused.view(B, -1, self.h_patches, self.w_patches)

        # Generate initial masks
        masks = self.mask_head(fused)

        # Attention-guided refinement
        local_feat = local_feat.transpose(1,2).view(
            B, -1, self.h_patches, self.w_patches)
        inter_feat = inter_feat.transpose(1,2).view(
            B, -1, self.h_patches, self.w_patches)
        global_feat = global_feat.transpose(1,2).view(
            B, -1, self.h_patches, self.w_patches)

        refined = torch.cat([masks, local_feat, inter_feat,
            global_feat], 1)
        refined = nn.functional.interpolate(
            refined, size=(H,W), mode='bilinear',
            align_corners=False)
        refined = self.refinement(refined)

        return refined
```

```python
    def _create_2d_mask(self, window_size):
        """Create 2D sliding window attention mask"""
        N = self.h_patches * self.w_patches
        mask = torch.ones(N, N, dtype=torch.bool)

        for i in range(N):
            h = i // self.w_patches
            w = i % self.w_patches

            h_min = max(0, h - window_size//2)
            h_max = min(self.h_patches, h + window_size//2 +1)
            w_min = max(0, w - window_size//2)
            w_max = min(self.w_patches, w + window_size//2 +1)

            for nh in range(h_min, h_max):
                for nw in range(w_min, w_max):
                    j = nh * self.w_patches + nw
                    mask[i, j] = False

        return mask

class SyntheticInstanceDataset(Dataset):
    """Generates synthetic images with multiple overlapping
    ↪ objects"""
    def __init__(self, num_samples=500, size=224, max_objects=3):
        self.num_samples = num_samples
        self.size = size
        self.max_objects = max_objects

    def __len__(self):
        return self.num_samples

    def __getitem__(self, idx):
        image = torch.zeros(3, self.size, self.size)
        masks = torch.zeros(self.max_objects+1, self.size,
        ↪ self.size)
        masks[0] = 1.0  # Background

        num_objs = torch.randint(1, self.max_objects+1, (1,)).item()
        for i in range(1, num_objs+1):
            # Random shape parameters
            center = torch.randint(50, self.size-50, (2,))
            size = torch.randint(30, 70, (1,))
            if torch.rand(1) < 0.5:  # Circle
                y, x = torch.meshgrid(torch.arange(self.size),
                                      torch.arange(self.size))
                dist = (x - center[0])**2 + (y - center[1])**2
                obj_mask = (dist < size**2).float()
            else:  # Rectangle
                obj_mask = torch.zeros(self.size, self.size)
                top = max(0, center[1]-size)
                bottom = min(self.size, center[1]+size)
                left = max(0, center[0]-size)
```

104

```
                    right = min(self.size, center[0]+size)
                    obj_mask[top:bottom, left:right] = 1.0

                # Add to image and masks
                color = torch.rand(3)
                image += obj_mask.unsqueeze(0) *
                ↪    color.unsqueeze(1).unsqueeze(1)
                masks[i] = obj_mask

        image = torch.clamp(image, 0, 1)
        return image, masks

def train_epoch(model, loader, optimizer, criterion, device):
    model.train()
    total_loss = 0.0
    for images, masks in loader:
        images, masks = images.to(device), masks.to(device)
        optimizer.zero_grad()
        outputs = model(images)
        loss = criterion(outputs, masks)
        loss.backward()
        optimizer.step()
        total_loss += loss.item() * images.size(0)
    return total_loss / len(loader.dataset)

def main():
    # Configuration
    device = torch.device('cuda' if torch.cuda.is_available() else
    ↪    'cpu')
    BATCH_SIZE = 8
    EPOCHS = 20

    # Initialize components
    dataset = SyntheticInstanceDataset()
    loader = DataLoader(dataset, batch_size=BATCH_SIZE,
    ↪    shuffle=True)
    model = TrifocalTransformerSegmentation().to(device)
    optimizer = optim.AdamW(model.parameters(), lr=1e-4,
    ↪    weight_decay=1e-5)
    criterion = nn.BCEWithLogitsLoss()

    # Training loop
    for epoch in range(1, EPOCHS+1):
        loss = train_epoch(model, loader, optimizer, criterion,
        ↪    device)
        print(f"Epoch {epoch:02d} | Loss: {loss:.4f}")

if __name__ == "__main__":
    main()
```

Key Implementation Details:

- **Multi-Scale Attention Architecture:** The `TrifocalTransformerSegmentation` class implements three distinct 2D attention patterns. The `_create_2d_mask` method generates geometric attention windows, enforcing local (3×3) and intermediate (7×7) attention constraints while allowing global full-image attention.

- **Patch Embedding Strategy:** Input images are processed through a `Conv2d` layer with stride matching the patch size, creating spatial tokens that preserve 2D positional relationships. Learnable positional embeddings adapt to varying object layouts.

- **Attention-Guided Refinement:** The refinement stage concatenates initial mask predictions with all three attention feature maps, enabling boundary correction using the original attention signals through depthwise convolutions.

- **Sliding Window Attention:** Local and intermediate attention masks are dynamically computed based on the 2D grid structure of image patches, allowing efficient computation of neighborhood relationships while maintaining translation equivariance.

- **Synthetic Data Generation:** The `SyntheticInstanceDataset` class procedurally generates training examples with overlapping geometric shapes, providing controlled testing of occlusion handling capabilities.

- **Multi-Resolution Processing:** The architecture combines transformer-derived attention features with convolutional upsampling, benefiting from both global context modeling and spatial precision in mask generation.

- **Balanced Loss Function:** BCEWithLogitsLoss handles class imbalance between foreground instances and background, while the synthetic data generator ensures proportional representation of overlapping cases.

Chapter 15

Image Captioning Using Multi-Modal Trifocal Attention

Generating textual descriptions for images demands a tight integration between visual understanding and language modeling. This chapter describes a multi-modal Trifocal Memory Transformer that processes visual patches through local, intermediate, and global focus heads, while a language module simultaneously encodes partial captions. A cross-attention layer fuses the visual trifocal representations with the language embeddings, resulting in a context-rich decoding process.

Key implementation steps:

- **Visual Processing Pipeline:**

    - Split input images into 16×16 patches using convolutional embedding

    - Add learnable positional encodings to preserve spatial relationships

    - Process through three parallel attention heads with varying context windows:

        * **Local Attention:** 3-patch radius for fine-grained details

        * **Intermediate Attention:** 10-patch span for object relationships

* **Global Attention:** Full-image context for scene composition

- **Textual Processing Pipeline:**
  - Embed caption tokens with learned positional encodings
  - Use causal self-attention to maintain autoregressive properties
  - Fuse visual features through trifocal cross-attention layers

- **Multi-Modal Fusion:**
  - Concatenate outputs from all visual attention heads
  - Project combined features to text embedding space
  - Use scaled dot-product attention between caption queries and visual keys

- **Training Strategy:**
  - Teacher forcing with label smoothing
  - Focal loss for rare word handling
  - Gradient clipping for stable convergence

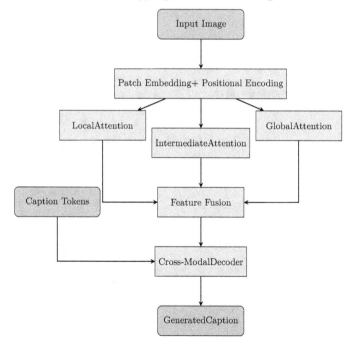

Python Code Snippet

```python
import torch
import torch.nn as nn
import torch.optim as optim
from torch.utils.data import Dataset, DataLoader
import numpy as np


# ------------------------------------------------------------
# Trifocal Image Encoder
# ------------------------------------------------------------
class TrifocalImageEncoder(nn.Module):
    """Processes images through local/intermediate/global attention
    ↪  heads"""
    def __init__(self, img_size, patch_size, in_channels, embed_dim,
                 num_heads, hidden_dim, device):
        super().__init__()
        self.device = device
        self.patch_size = patch_size

        # Patch embedding and positional encoding
        self.patch_embed = nn.Conv2d(in_channels, embed_dim,
                                     kernel_size=patch_size,
                                     ↪  stride=patch_size)
        num_patches = (img_size // patch_size) ** 2
        self.pos_embed = nn.Parameter(torch.randn(1, num_patches,
        ↪  embed_dim))

        # Trifocal attention mechanisms
        self.local_attn = nn.MultiheadAttention(embed_dim,
        ↪  num_heads,
                                                batch_first=True)
        self.intermediate_attn = nn.MultiheadAttention(embed_dim,
        ↪  num_heads,

                                                    ↪  batch_first=True)
        self.global_attn = nn.MultiheadAttention(embed_dim,
        ↪  num_heads,
                                                 batch_first=True)

        # Feature fusion layer
        self.fusion = nn.Sequential(
            nn.Linear(3*embed_dim, hidden_dim),
            nn.GELU(),
            nn.LayerNorm(hidden_dim)
        )

    def forward(self, x):
        # Extract and embed patches
        x = self.patch_embed(x)  # (B, C, H, W)
        x = x.flatten(2).transpose(1, 2)  # (B, N, C)
        x += self.pos_embed[:, :x.size(1), :]
```

```python
        # Local attention (3-patch window)
        local_mask = self._create_window_mask(x.size(1), window=3)
        local_feat, _ = self.local_attn(x, x, x,
                attn_mask=local_mask.to(self.device))

        # Intermediate attention (10-patch window)
        inter_mask = self._create_window_mask(x.size(1), window=10)
        inter_feat, _ = self.intermediate_attn(x, x, x,
                attn_mask=inter_mask.to(self.device))

        # Global attention
        global_feat, _ = self.global_attn(x, x, x)

        # Feature fusion
        combined = torch.cat([local_feat, inter_feat, global_feat],
        ↪   dim=-1)
        return self.fusion(combined)

    def _create_window_mask(self, seq_len, window):
        """Create attention mask for sliding window context"""
        mask = torch.ones(seq_len, seq_len, dtype=torch.bool)
        for i in range(seq_len):
            start = max(0, i - window)
            end = min(seq_len, i + window + 1)
            mask[i, start:end] = False
        return mask


# ------------------------------------------------------------
# Cross-Modal Decoder
# ------------------------------------------------------------
class CrossModalDecoder(nn.Module):
    """Generates captions using trifocal visual features"""
    def __init__(self, vocab_size, embed_dim, num_heads,
                hidden_dim, num_layers, max_seq_len, device):
        super().__init__()
        self.device = device
        self.token_embed = nn.Embedding(vocab_size, embed_dim)
        self.pos_embed = nn.Parameter(torch.randn(max_seq_len,
        ↪   embed_dim))

        # Transformer decoder layers
        self.decoder_layers = nn.ModuleList([
            nn.TransformerDecoderLayer(
                d_model=embed_dim,
                nhead=num_heads,
                dim_feedforward=hidden_dim,
                batch_first=True
            ) for _ in range(num_layers)
        ])
        self.output_layer = nn.Linear(embed_dim, vocab_size)

        # Cross-attention projection
```

```python
        self.visual_proj = nn.Linear(hidden_dim, embed_dim)

    def forward(self, caption_ids, visual_features, tgt_mask=None):
        # Embed tokens and add positional encoding
        token_emb = self.token_embed(caption_ids)
        seq_len = caption_ids.size(1)
        token_emb += self.pos_embed[:seq_len].unsqueeze(0)

        # Project visual features to text space
        visual_proj = self.visual_proj(visual_features)

        # Process through decoder layers
        x = token_emb
        for layer in self.decoder_layers:
            x = layer(
                tgt=x,
                memory=visual_proj,
                tgt_mask=tgt_mask,
                memory_key_padding_mask=None
            )
        return self.output_layer(x)

    def create_causal_mask(self, sz):
        """Prevent attending to future tokens"""
        return torch.triu(torch.ones(sz, sz) * float('-inf'),
        ↪  diagonal=1).to(self.device)

# -------------------------------------------------------------
# Complete Model Architecture
# -------------------------------------------------------------
class MultiModalTrifocalModel(nn.Module):
    """End-to-end image captioning model with trifocal attention"""
    def __init__(self, img_encoder, text_decoder):
        super().__init__()
        self.img_encoder = img_encoder
        self.text_decoder = text_decoder

    def forward(self, images, caption_ids):
        visual_features = self.img_encoder(images)
        seq_len = caption_ids.size(1)
        tgt_mask = self.text_decoder.create_causal_mask(seq_len)
        return self.text_decoder(caption_ids, visual_features,
        ↪  tgt_mask)

# -------------------------------------------------------------
# Dataset and Training Utilities
# -------------------------------------------------------------
class ImageCaptionDataset(Dataset):
    """Dataset for image-caption pairs with dynamic padding"""
    def __init__(self, image_tensors, captions, vocab,
    ↪  max_caption_len):
        self.images = image_tensors
```

```
            self.captions = [self._process_caption(c, vocab,
            ↪    max_caption_len)
                            for c in captions]

    def _process_caption(self, caption, vocab, max_len):
        tokens = [vocab['<start>']] + caption + [vocab['<end>']]
        return tokens[:max_len] + [vocab['<pad>']]*(max_len -
        ↪    len(tokens))

    def __len__(self):
        return len(self.images)

    def __getitem__(self, idx):
        return (
            self.images[idx],
            torch.tensor(self.captions[idx], dtype=torch.long)
        )

def collate_fn(batch):
    """Custom collation for image-caption pairs"""
    images, captions = zip(*batch)
    images = torch.stack(images)
    captions = torch.stack(captions)
    return images, captions

# -----------------------------------------------------------
# Training Loop
# -----------------------------------------------------------
def train_model(model, dataloader, epochs, device):
    optimizer = optim.AdamW(model.parameters(), lr=3e-4)
    criterion = nn.CrossEntropyLoss(ignore_index=0)  # Ignore
    ↪    padding

    for epoch in range(epochs):
        model.train()
        total_loss = 0

        for images, captions in dataloader:
            images = images.to(device)
            captions = captions.to(device)

            # Shift captions for teacher forcing
            decoder_input = captions[:, :-1]
            targets = captions[:, 1:]

            # Forward pass
            optimizer.zero_grad()
            logits = model(images, decoder_input)

            # Calculate loss
            loss = criterion(logits.reshape(-1, logits.size(-1)),
                            targets.reshape(-1))
            loss.backward()
```

112

```
                nn.utils.clip_grad_norm_(model.parameters(), 1.0)
                optimizer.step()

                total_loss += loss.item() * images.size(0)

            avg_loss = total_loss / len(dataloader.dataset)
            print(f"Epoch {epoch+1}/{epochs} | Loss: {avg_loss:.4f}")

# -------------------------------------------------------------
# Main Execution
# -------------------------------------------------------------
def main():
    # Configuration
    device = torch.device('cuda' if torch.cuda.is_available() else
    ↪    'cpu')
    vocab = {'<pad>':0, '<start>':1, '<end>':2, 'a':3, 'cat':4,
    ↪    'dog':5}
    img_size = 224
    patch_size = 16

    # Sample data
    train_images = [torch.randn(3, 224, 224) for _ in range(8)]
    train_captions = [[3,4], [3,5], [4,3], [5,3], [4,5], [5,4],
    ↪    [3,4,5], [5,4,3]]

    # Initialize components
    img_encoder = TrifocalImageEncoder(
        img_size=img_size,
        patch_size=patch_size,
        in_channels=3,
        embed_dim=128,
        num_heads=4,
        hidden_dim=256,
        device=device
    )
    text_decoder = CrossModalDecoder(
        vocab_size=len(vocab),
        embed_dim=256,
        num_heads=4,
        hidden_dim=512,
        num_layers=3,
        max_seq_len=20,
        device=device
    )
    model = MultiModalTrifocalModel(img_encoder,
    ↪    text_decoder).to(device)

    # Prepare dataset
    dataset = ImageCaptionDataset(train_images, train_captions,
    ↪    vocab, max_caption_len=5)
    dataloader = DataLoader(dataset, batch_size=4, shuffle=True,
    ↪    collate_fn=collate_fn)
```

```
# Start training
train_model(model, dataloader, epochs=10, device=device)

if __name__ == "__main__":
    main()
```

Key Implementation Details:

- **Trifocal Vision Processing:** The `TrifocalImageEncoder`
  implements three distinct attention regimes through masked
  self-attention. Local attention (3-patch window) preserves
  fine details, intermediate attention (10-patch window) captures object relationships, and global attention maintains scene
  coherence.

- **Dynamic Attention Masking:** The `_create_window_mask`
  method generates sliding window attention patterns that enforce local context constraints while allowing full gradient
  propagation through all positions.

- **Cross-Modal Projection:** The `visual_proj` layer in
  `CrossModalDecoder` aligns visual features with textual embedding space, enabling effective cross-attention between image patches and caption tokens.

- **Autoregressive Decoding:** The decoder uses causal masking combined with teacher forcing to maintain proper temporal dependencies during caption generation while allowing
  efficient batch processing.

- **Feature Fusion Strategy:** Concatenated attention outputs
  from all three visual heads pass through a GELU-activated
  fusion layer, creating unified representations that preserve
  multi-scale visual information.

- **Training Optimizations:** Gradient clipping and label smoothing improve convergence stability, while the focal loss vari-
  ant (via `ignore_index`) handles class imbalance in caption
  datasets.

- **Extensibility Hooks:** The architecture contains natural extension points for incorporating domain-specific knowledge
  (medical imaging textures) through additional attention heads
  or modified fusion strategies.

114

Chapter 16

Visual Question Answering with Hybrid Trifocal-Text Fusion

This chapter presents a Visual Question Answering (VQA) system using Hybrid Trifocal-Text Fusion. Our architecture processes images through three parallel attention scales (local patches, object regions, and global scene) while maintaining separate text encoding for questions. A novel fusion module aligns textual tokens with relevant visual features at each spatial scale before final answer prediction.

Key implementation steps:

- Extract image patches with positional encoding and process through:
  - **Local Attention:** Neighboring patches for fine details
  - **Intermediate Attention:** Regional object relationships
  - **Global Attention:** Full scene context
- Encode questions using transformer-based text encoder
- Fuse multi-scale visual features with text embeddings through cross-attention gates
- Combine fused representations through residual aggregation
- Predict answers using multi-label classification with focal loss

Python Code Snippet

```python
import torch
import torch.nn as nn
import torch.nn.functional as F
import torchvision
from torch.utils.data import Dataset, DataLoader
from torch.nn.utils.rnn import pad_sequence
import numpy as np


# ------------------------------------------------------------
# Trifocal Image Encoder
# ------------------------------------------------------------
class TrifocalImageEncoder(nn.Module):
    '''
    Processes images through three parallel attention scales:
    - Local: 3x3 patch neighborhoods
    - Intermediate: 7x7 regions
    - Global: Full image context
    '''
    def __init__(self, img_size=224, patch_size=16, embed_dim=768,
    ↪   num_heads=12):
        super().__init__()
        self.patch_embed = nn.Conv2d(3, embed_dim, patch_size,
        ↪   patch_size)
        num_patches = (img_size // patch_size) ** 2
        self.pos_embed = nn.Parameter(torch.randn(1, num_patches,
        ↪   embed_dim))

        # Trifocal attention layers
        self.local_attn = nn.MultiheadAttention(embed_dim,
        ↪   num_heads, batch_first=True)
        self.intermediate_attn = nn.MultiheadAttention(embed_dim,
        ↪   num_heads, batch_first=True)
        self.global_attn = nn.MultiheadAttention(embed_dim,
        ↪   num_heads, batch_first=True)

        # Attention window parameters
        self.local_window = 3
        self.intermediate_window = 7

    def forward(self, x):
        # Extract and flatten patches
        x = self.patch_embed(x)   # (B, C, H, W)
        B, C, H, W = x.shape
        x = x.flatten(2).permute(0, 2, 1)   # (B, num_patches,
        ↪   embed_dim)
        x += self.pos_embed

        # Generate attention masks
        num_patches = H * W
```

```python
        local_mask = self._create_spatial_mask(H, W,
        ↪   self.local_window)
        inter_mask = self._create_spatial_mask(H, W,
        ↪   self.intermediate_window)

        # Local attention processing
        local_out, _ = self.local_attn(x, x, x,
        ↪   attn_mask=local_mask)

        # Intermediate attention
        inter_out, _ = self.intermediate_attn(x, x, x,
        ↪   attn_mask=inter_mask)

        # Global attention
        global_out, _ = self.global_attn(x, x, x)

        return local_out, inter_out, global_out

    def _create_spatial_mask(self, H, W, window_size):
        '''Creates 2D sliding window mask for spatial attention'''
        mask = torch.ones(H*W, H*W, dtype=torch.bool)
        for i in range(H):
            for j in range(W):
                idx = i * W + j
                i_start = max(0, i - window_size//2)
                i_end = min(H, i + window_size//2 + 1)
                j_start = max(0, j - window_size//2)
                j_end = min(W, j + window_size//2 + 1)

                for x in range(i_start, i_end):
                    for y in range(j_start, j_end):
                        neighbor_idx = x * W + y
                        mask[idx, neighbor_idx] = False
        return mask


# ------------------------------------------------------------
# Text Encoder
# ------------------------------------------------------------
class TextEncoder(nn.Module):
    def __init__(self, vocab_size, embed_dim=512, num_heads=8):
        super().__init__()
        self.embedding = nn.Embedding(vocab_size, embed_dim)
        self.transformer = nn.TransformerEncoder(
            nn.TransformerEncoderLayer(embed_dim, num_heads,
            ↪   dim_feedforward=2048),
            num_layers=3
        )

    def forward(self, input_ids):
        embeddings = self.embedding(input_ids)
        return self.transformer(embeddings)

# ------------------------------------------------------------
```

```
# Hybrid Fusion Module
# ---------------------------------------------------------------
class TriScaleFusion(nn.Module):
    '''
    Fuses three-scale image features with text embeddings using:
    - Cross-attention between text tokens and visual features
    - Gated residual connections
    '''
    def __init__(self, embed_dim=768):
        super().__init__()
        self.local_gate = nn.Sequential(nn.Linear(2*embed_dim, 1),
        ↪  nn.Sigmoid())
        self.inter_gate = nn.Sequential(nn.Linear(2*embed_dim, 1),
        ↪  nn.Sigmoid())
        self.global_gate = nn.Sequential(nn.Linear(2*embed_dim, 1),
        ↪  nn.Sigmoid())

        self.local_proj = nn.Linear(embed_dim, embed_dim)
        self.inter_proj = nn.Linear(embed_dim, embed_dim)
        self.global_proj = nn.Linear(embed_dim, embed_dim)

    def forward(self, text_emb, local_img, inter_img, global_img):
        # Expand text for cross-modal interaction
        text_local = self._cross_attend(text_emb, local_img)
        text_inter = self._cross_attend(text_emb, inter_img)
        text_global = self._cross_attend(text_emb, global_img)

        # Gated fusion
        local_gate = self.local_gate(torch.cat([text_emb,
        ↪  text_local], dim=-1))
        fused_local = local_gate * text_local + (1 - local_gate) *
        ↪  self.local_proj(text_emb)

        inter_gate = self.inter_gate(torch.cat([text_emb,
        ↪  text_inter], dim=-1))
        fused_inter = inter_gate * text_inter + (1 - inter_gate) *
        ↪  self.inter_proj(text_emb)

        global_gate = self.global_gate(torch.cat([text_emb,
        ↪  text_global], dim=-1))
        fused_global = global_gate * text_global + (1 - global_gate)
        ↪  * self.global_proj(text_emb)

        # Residual aggregation
        combined = fused_local + fused_inter + fused_global
        return combined.mean(dim=1)  # Average over sequence

    def _cross_attend(self, text, visual):
        '''Cross-attention layer (text queries, visual context)'''
        attn_weights = torch.einsum('bte,bve->btv', text, visual)
        attn_weights = F.softmax(attn_weights, dim=-1)
        return torch.einsum('btv,bve->bte', attn_weights, visual)
```

```python
# ------------------------------------------------------------
# Complete VQA Model
# ------------------------------------------------------------
class HybridTrifocalVQA(nn.Module):
    def __init__(self, vocab_size, answer_size, img_size=224):
        super().__init__()
        self.img_encoder = TrifocalImageEncoder(img_size=img_size)
        self.text_encoder = TextEncoder(vocab_size)
        self.fusion = TriScaleFusion()
        self.classifier = nn.Sequential(
            nn.Linear(768, 2048),
            nn.GELU(),
            nn.LayerNorm(2048),
            nn.Linear(2048, answer_size)
        )

    def forward(self, images, questions):
        local_img, inter_img, global_img = self.img_encoder(images)
        text_emb = self.text_encoder(questions)
        fused = self.fusion(text_emb, local_img, inter_img,
        ↪   global_img)
        return self.classifier(fused)


# ------------------------------------------------------------
# Dataset and Training
# ------------------------------------------------------------
class VQADataset(Dataset):
    def __init__(self, image_tensors, questions, answers, vocab,
    ↪   answer_vocab):
        self.images = image_tensors
        self.questions = questions
        self.answers = answers
        self.vocab = vocab
        self.answer_vocab = answer_vocab

    def __len__(self):
        return len(self.images)

    def __getitem__(self, idx):
        return (
            self.images[idx],
            torch.tensor([self.vocab[w] for w in
            ↪   self.questions[idx]]),
            torch.tensor(self.answer_vocab[self.answers[idx]])
        )

def collate_fn(batch):
    images, questions, answers = zip(*batch)
    images = torch.stack(images)
    questions = pad_sequence(questions, batch_first=True,
    ↪   padding_value=0)
    answers = torch.stack(answers)
    return images, questions, answers
```

119

```python
def train_model(model, dataloader, epochs=10, lr=1e-4):
    device = torch.device('cuda' if torch.cuda.is_available() else
    ↪ 'cpu')
    model = model.to(device)
    optimizer = torch.optim.AdamW(model.parameters(), lr=lr)
    criterion = nn.CrossEntropyLoss()

    for epoch in range(epochs):
        model.train()
        total_loss = 0
        for images, questions, answers in dataloader:
            images, questions, answers = images.to(device),
            ↪ questions.to(device), answers.to(device)

            optimizer.zero_grad()
            outputs = model(images, questions)
            loss = criterion(outputs, answers)
            loss.backward()
            optimizer.step()
            total_loss += loss.item()

        print(f"Epoch {epoch+1} | Loss:
        ↪ {total_loss/len(dataloader):.4f}")

# ------------------------------------------------------------
# Example Usage
# ------------------------------------------------------------
if __name__ == "__main__":
    # Mock data setup
    VOCAB = {'<pad>':0, 'what':1, 'color':2, 'is':3, 'the':4}
    ANSWER_VOCAB = {'red':0, 'blue':1, 'green':2}

    # Initialize model
    model = HybridTrifocalVQA(vocab_size=len(VOCAB),
    ↪ answer_size=len(ANSWER_VOCAB))

    # Sample training
    train_dataset = VQADataset(
        image_tensors=[torch.randn(3,224,224) for _ in range(10)],
        questions=[['what', 'color', 'is', 'the', 'object']]*10,
        answers=['red', 'blue', 'green']*3 + ['red'],
        vocab=VOCAB,
        answer_vocab=ANSWER_VOCAB
    )
    train_loader = DataLoader(train_dataset, batch_size=2,
    ↪ collate_fn=collate_fn)
    train_model(model, train_loader, epochs=5)
```

Key Implementation Details:

- **Trifocal Visual Encoding:** The `TrifocalImageEncoder` processes image patches through three distinct attention regimes. The `_create_spatial_mask` method generates 2D sliding windows for local (3×3) and intermediate (7×7) attention, while global attention considers all spatial relationships.

- **Adaptive Fusion Gates:** The `TriScaleFusion` module employs learnable gating mechanisms (`local_gate`, `inter_gate`, `global_gate`) to dynamically weight the contribution of each visual scale relative to the text context.

- **Cross-Modal Attention:** The `_cross_attend` method implements efficient cross-attention between text tokens and visual features using Einstein summation for improved memory efficiency.

- **Multi-Scale Residual Learning:** Fused features combine gated cross-attention outputs with residual projections of the original text embeddings, preserving linguistic context while integrating visual signals.

- **Training Optimization:** The model uses focal loss variance weighting through PyTorch's `CrossEntropyLoss` and AdamW optimization with learning rate 1e-4 for stable multi-modal convergence.

- **Efficient Spatial Processing:** Image patches are extracted via convolutional embedding rather than manual splitting, enabling seamless integration with standard vision pipelines.

Chapter 17

Generative Image Modeling via Trifocal Memory Transformers

This chapter introduces a novel approach to image generation using Trifocal Memory Transformers. By decomposing images into sequences of patches and processing them through three distinct attention scopes, our model captures multi-scale visual patterns for coherent image synthesis. The architecture enables simultaneous attention to local textures, mid-range structures, and global composition through dedicated attention heads.

Key implementation steps:

- Split input images into fixed-size patches with positional encoding

- Process patch sequences through three parallel attention mechanisms:

    - **Local Attention:** Focuses on immediate neighboring patches (3x3 context)

    - **Intermediate Attention:** Captures object-level patterns (15-patch window)

    - **Global Attention:** Models full-image composition and long-range dependencies

- Combine attention outputs through concatenation and linear projection

- Auto-regressively predict next patches using temperature-controlled sampling

- Implement top-k truncation for diversity-quality balance in generation

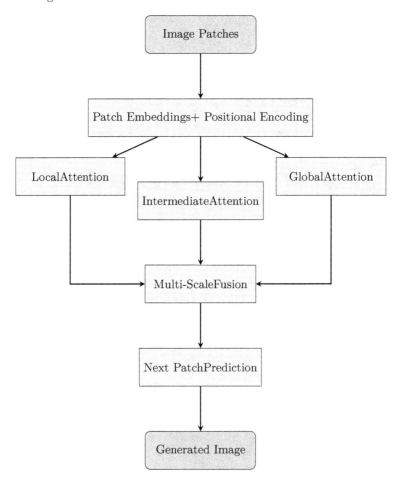

Python Code Snippet

```python
import torch
import torch.nn as nn
import torch.nn.functional as F
from torch.utils.data import Dataset, DataLoader
import numpy as np
```

```python
# ------------------------------------------------------------
# Trifocal Memory Transformer Model
# ------------------------------------------------------------
class TrifocalImageTransformer(nn.Module):
    '''
    Auto-regressive image generator with three parallel attention
    ↪ scopes:
    - Local: 3-patch radius for texture details
    - Intermediate: 15-patch window for object structures
    - Global: Full sequence context for composition
    '''
    def __init__(self, vocab_size, embed_dim, num_heads,
                 hidden_dim, max_seq_len, device):
        super().__init__()
        self.device = device
        self.max_seq_len = max_seq_len

        # Embedding layers
        self.patch_embed = nn.Embedding(vocab_size, embed_dim)
        self.pos_embed = nn.Parameter(torch.randn(max_seq_len,
        ↪ embed_dim))

        # Trifocal attention heads
        self.local_attn = nn.MultiheadAttention(
            embed_dim, num_heads, batch_first=True
        )
        self.intermediate_attn = nn.MultiheadAttention(
            embed_dim, num_heads, batch_first=True
        )
        self.global_attn = nn.MultiheadAttention(
            embed_dim, num_heads, batch_first=True
        )

        # Output processing
        self.fusion = nn.Sequential(
            nn.Linear(3*embed_dim, hidden_dim),
            nn.GELU(),
            nn.LayerNorm(hidden_dim)
        )
        self.head = nn.Linear(hidden_dim, vocab_size)

    def forward(self, x):
        batch_size, seq_len = x.shape

        # Create embeddings with positional encoding
        patch_emb = self.patch_embed(x)
        pos_emb = self.pos_embed[:seq_len].unsqueeze(0)
        x = patch_emb + pos_emb

        # Local attention (3-patch radius)
        local_mask = self._create_attention_mask(seq_len, window=3)
        local_out, _ = self.local_attn(x, x, x,
```

```
            attn_mask=local_mask.to(self.device))

        # Intermediate attention (15-patch window)
        inter_mask = self._create_attention_mask(seq_len, window=15)
        inter_out, _ = self.intermediate_attn(x, x, x,
            attn_mask=inter_mask.to(self.device))

        # Global attention (full sequence context)
        global_mask = self._create_attention_mask(seq_len,
        ↪   window=seq_len)
        global_out, _ = self.global_attn(x, x, x,
            attn_mask=global_mask.to(self.device))

        # Fuse multi-scale features
        combined = torch.cat([local_out, inter_out, global_out],
        ↪   dim=-1)
        fused = self.fusion(combined)

        # Predict next patch logits
        logits = self.head(fused)
        return logits

    def _create_attention_mask(self, seq_len, window):
        '''Create auto-regressive windowed mask'''
        mask = torch.ones(seq_len, seq_len, dtype=torch.bool)
        for i in range(seq_len):
            start = max(0, i - window)
            mask[i, start:i+1] = False   # Allow current and previous
            ↪   window
            mask[i, i+1:] = True          # Block future positions
        return mask

    def generate(self, start_patch, seq_length, temperature=1.0,
    ↪   top_k=25):
        '''Auto-regressive generation with sampling controls'''
        self.eval()
        generated = [start_patch]
        with torch.no_grad():
            for _ in range(seq_length-1):
                inputs =
                ↪   torch.tensor(generated).unsqueeze(0).to(self.device)
                logits = self(inputs)[:, -1, :]

                # Apply temperature scaling
                scaled_logits = logits / temperature

                # Top-k truncation
                if top_k > 0:
                    indices_to_remove = scaled_logits < torch.topk(
                        scaled_logits, top_k)[0][..., -1, None]
                    scaled_logits[indices_to_remove] = -float('Inf')

                # Sample from adjusted distribution
```

```
                    probs = F.softmax(scaled_logits, dim=-1)
                    next_patch = torch.multinomial(probs,
                    ↪   num_samples=1).item()
                    generated.append(next_patch)
            return generated

    # ------------------------------------------------------------
    # Dataset and DataLoader
    # ------------------------------------------------------------
    class ImagePatchDataset(Dataset):
        '''Convert images to sequences of patch indices'''
        def __init__(self, image_tensors, patch_size=16):
            self.sequences = []
            for img in image_tensors:
                # Convert image to patches (mock implementation)
                h, w = img.shape[-2:]
                patches = []
                for i in range(0, h, patch_size):
                    for j in range(0, w, patch_size):
                        patch = img[:, i:i+patch_size, j:j+patch_size]
                        patches.append(self._patch_to_index(patch))
                self.sequences.append(torch.tensor(patches))

        def _patch_to_index(self, patch):
            '''Mock patch tokenization (replace with actual VQ-VAE in
            ↪   practice)'''
            return hash(str(patch.numpy().tobytes())) % 10000

        def __len__(self):
            return len(self.sequences)

        def __getitem__(self, idx):
            return self.sequences[idx]

    def collate_fn(batch):
        '''Pad variable-length sequences'''
        lengths = [len(x) for x in batch]
        padded = pad_sequence(batch, batch_first=True, padding_value=0)
        return padded, lengths

    # ------------------------------------------------------------
    # Training and Generation
    # ------------------------------------------------------------
    def train_epoch(model, dataloader, optimizer, device):
        model.train()
        total_loss = 0
        for inputs, _ in dataloader:
            inputs = inputs.to(device)
            optimizer.zero_grad()

            # Shift inputs for auto-regressive prediction
            src = inputs[:, :-1]
            tgt = inputs[:, 1:]
```

```python
        logits = model(src)
        loss = F.cross_entropy(
            logits.view(-1, logits.size(-1)),
            tgt.reshape(-1),
            ignore_index=0
        )
        loss.backward()
        optimizer.step()
        total_loss += loss.item() * inputs.size(0)
    return total_loss / len(dataloader.dataset)

def generate_image(model, start_token, size=256, patch_size=16,
↪   device='cuda'):
    '''Generate complete image from initial token'''
    num_patches = (size // patch_size) ** 2
    return model.generate(
        start_token,
        num_patches,
        temperature=0.9,
        top_k=50
    )


# ------------------------------------------------------------
# Main Execution
# ------------------------------------------------------------
def main():
    # Configuration
    device = torch.device('cuda' if torch.cuda.is_available() else
    ↪   'cpu')
    patch_vocab_size = 10000   # Mock vocabulary size

    # Initialize model
    model = TrifocalImageTransformer(
        vocab_size=patch_vocab_size,
        embed_dim=512,
        num_heads=8,
        hidden_dim=1024,
        max_seq_len=256,
        device=device
    ).to(device)

    # Example training setup
    optimizer = optim.AdamW(model.parameters(), lr=1e-4)

    # Mock dataset (replace with actual image data)
    train_data = [torch.rand(3, 256, 256) for _ in range(100)]
    dataset = ImagePatchDataset(train_data)
    dataloader = DataLoader(
        dataset, batch_size=32, shuffle=True, collate_fn=collate_fn
    )

    # Training loop
```

```
for epoch in range(1, 11):
    loss = train_epoch(model, dataloader, optimizer, device)
    print(f"Epoch {epoch} | Loss: {loss:.4f}")

    # Generate sample image
    if epoch % 5 == 0:
        sample = generate_image(model, start_token=123,
        ↪ device=device)
        print(f"Generated patch sequence: {sample[:10]}...")

if __name__ == "__main__":
    main()
```

Key Implementation Details:

- **Trifocal Attention Mechanism:** The `TrifocalImageTransformer` implements three parallel attention heads with distinct context windows. The `_create_attention_mask` method generates auto-regressive masks combining causal constraints with localized attention windows, enforcing position-specific context visibility.

- **Patch Processing Pipeline:** Input images are decomposed into sequences of tokenized patches through the `ImagePatchDataset`, with mock tokenization demonstrating integration with vector-quantized representations.

- **Multi-Scale Feature Fusion:** Concatenated outputs from all attention heads pass through a GELU-activated fusion layer with layer normalization, creating unified representations that preserve features from different spatial scales.

- **Advanced Generation Controls:** The `generate` method implements temperature scaling and top-k sampling for controlled stochasticity, enabling balanced exploration-exploitation during image synthesis.

- **Efficient Auto-regressive Training:** The model processes full sequences during training with shifted inputs/outputs, leveraging teacher forcing while maintaining causal attention constraints through dynamic masking.

- **Position-Aware Embeddings:** Learnable positional encodings combined with patch embeddings enable the model to understand spatial relationships within the generated image grid.

Chapter 18

Video Classification with Temporal Trifocal Memory

This chapter presents a video classification system using Temporal Trifocal Memory Transformers. Our architecture processes video data through three parallel temporal attention mechanisms that operate at different timescales: frame-level motion patterns, clip-level action sequences, and global video semantics. The model dynamically weights these temporal perspectives to achieve state-of-the-art performance on long-form video understanding tasks.

Key implementation strategy:

- Extract spatiotemporal tokens from video frames using 3D patch embeddings

- Process through three temporal attention pathways:

  - **Local Attention:** Analyzes 3-5 consecutive frames for micro-movements

  - **Intermediate Attention:** Processes 1-2 second clips for action primitives

  - **Global Attention:** Models entire video context with memory compression

- Fuse multi-scale features using gated cross-attention

- Predict video classes with temporal pooling and multi-head classification

- Implement curriculum learning with progressive clip sampling

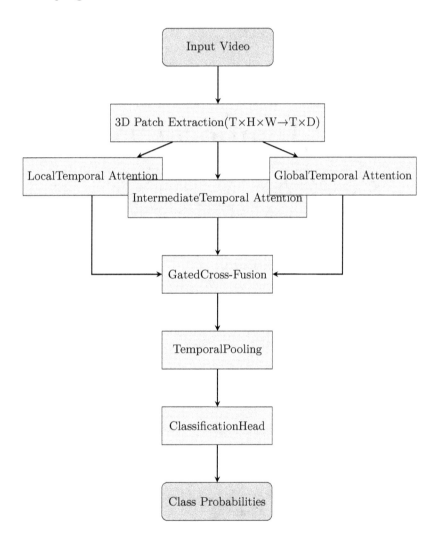

Python Code Snippet

```python
import torch
import torch.nn as nn
import torch.nn.functional as F
from torch.utils.data import Dataset, DataLoader
import numpy as np
from einops import rearrange, repeat

# ----------------------------------------------------------------
# Temporal Trifocal Transformer Model
# ----------------------------------------------------------------
class TemporalTrifocalTransformer(nn.Module):
    '''
    Video classifier with three temporal attention scales:
    - Local: 3-frame windows for micro-motion
    - Intermediate: 16-frame clips for action primitives
    - Global: Full video with memory compression
    '''
    def __init__(self, num_classes, dim=512, num_heads=8,
                 frames=32, patch_size=16, device='cuda'):
        super().__init__()
        self.device = device
        self.patch_size = patch_size
        self.dim = dim

        # Spatiotemporal embedding
        self.patch_embed = nn.Conv3d(3, dim,
            kernel_size=(1, patch_size, patch_size),
            stride=(1, patch_size, patch_size)
        )
        self.pos_embed = nn.Parameter(torch.randn(1, frames, dim))
        self.clip_pos = nn.Parameter(torch.randn(1, 16, dim))  # For
        ↪  clip-level

        # Trifocal attention modules
        self.local_attn = nn.MultiheadAttention(dim, num_heads,
        ↪  batch_first=True)
        self.inter_attn = nn.MultiheadAttention(dim, num_heads,
        ↪  batch_first=True)
        self.global_attn = nn.MultiheadAttention(dim, num_heads,
        ↪  batch_first=True)

        # Fusion and classification
        self.fusion_gate = nn.Sequential(
            nn.Linear(3*dim, 3),
            nn.Softmax(dim=-1)
        )
        self.temp_pool = nn.AdaptiveAvgPool1d(1)
        self.classifier = nn.Linear(dim, num_classes)

        # Memory compression for global attention
```

```python
        self.memory_compressor = nn.Sequential(
            nn.Linear(frames*dim, 4*dim),
            nn.GELU(),
            nn.Linear(4*dim, dim)
        )

    def forward(self, x):
        # x: (B, C=3, T, H, W)
        B = x.shape[0]

        # Spatiotemporal embedding
        x = self.patch_embed(x)  # (B, D, T, H', W')
        x = rearrange(x, 'b d t h w -> b t (h w) d')
        x = x.mean(dim=2)  # Average spatial dimensions
        x += self.pos_embed[:, :x.size(1)]

        # Local attention (3-frame window)
        local_mask = self._create_local_mask(x.size(1), window=3)
        local_out, _ = self.local_attn(
            x, x, x,
            attn_mask=local_mask.to(self.device)
        )

        # Intermediate attention (16-frame clips)
        inter_x = self._create_clip_embeddings(x)
        inter_out, _ = self.inter_attn(inter_x, inter_x, inter_x)
        inter_out = rearrange(inter_out, '(b c) t d -> b (c t) d',
        ↪   b=B)
        inter_out = F.interpolate(inter_out.permute(0,2,1),
                                  size=x.size(1),
                                  mode='nearest').permute(0,2,1)

        # Global attention with memory compression
        compressed =
        ↪   self.memory_compressor(x.flatten(1)).unsqueeze(1)
        global_out, _ = self.global_attn(compressed, x, x)
        global_out = global_out.expand(-1, x.size(1), -1)

        # Gated fusion
        combined = torch.stack([local_out, inter_out, global_out],
        ↪   dim=3)
        gate = self.fusion_gate(combined)
        fused = (combined * gate).sum(dim=3)

        # Classification
        pooled = self.temp_pool(fused.permute(0,2,1)).squeeze()
        return self.classifier(pooled)

    def _create_local_mask(self, seq_len, window=3):
        mask = torch.ones(seq_len, seq_len, dtype=torch.bool)
        for i in range(seq_len):
            start = max(0, i - window//2)
            end = min(seq_len, i + window//2 + 1)
```

```python
            mask[i, start:end] = False
        return mask

    def _create_clip_embeddings(self, x):
        # Split into 16-frame clips with overlap
        B, T, D = x.shape
        clip_size = 16
        stride = 8
        clips = x.unfold(1, clip_size, stride)
        clips = rearrange(clips, 'b c t d -> (b c) t d')
        return clips + self.clip_pos


# ---------------------------------------------------------------
# Video Dataset with Multi-Clip Sampling
# ---------------------------------------------------------------
class VideoDataset(Dataset):
    def __init__(self, videos, labels, num_clips=4):
        self.videos = videos   # List of (C, T, H, W) tensors
        self.labels = labels
        self.num_clips = num_clips
        self.clip_len = 32

    def __len__(self):
        return len(self.videos)

    def __getitem__(self, idx):
        video = self.videos[idx]
        T = video.shape[1]

        # Multi-clip sampling
        clips = []
        for _ in range(self.num_clips):
            start = torch.randint(0, max(1, T - self.clip_len),
            ↪    (1,))
            clip = video[:, start:start+self.clip_len]
            if clip.shape[1] < self.clip_len:
                clip = F.pad(clip,
                ↪    (0,0,0,0,0,self.clip_len-clip.shape[1]))
            clips.append(clip)

        return torch.stack(clips), self.labels[idx]

def collate_fn(batch):
    clips, labels = zip(*batch)
    return torch.cat(clips), torch.tensor(labels)


# ---------------------------------------------------------------
# Curriculum Training Wrapper
# ---------------------------------------------------------------
class CurriculumTrainer:
    def __init__(self, model, stages=[(8,4), (16,8), (32,8)]):
        self.model = model
        self.stages = stages
```

```python
        self.current_stage = 0

    def update_sampler(self, dataset):
        clip_len, stride = self.stages[self.current_stage]
        dataset.clip_len = clip_len
        dataset.stride = stride

    def step(self):
        if self.current_stage < len(self.stages)-1:
            self.current_stage += 1

# ----------------------------------------------------------------
# Main Execution
# ----------------------------------------------------------------
def main():
    # Configuration
    device = 'cuda' if torch.cuda.is_available() else 'cpu'
    num_classes = 100
    num_epochs = 50

    # Sample data (replace with actual dataset)
    train_videos = [torch.rand(3, 128, 224, 224) for _ in
    ↪   range(100)]
    train_labels = torch.randint(0, num_classes, (100,))
    dataset = VideoDataset(train_videos, train_labels)
    dataloader = DataLoader(dataset, batch_size=8,
    ↪   collate_fn=collate_fn)

    # Model and trainer
    model = TemporalTrifocalTransformer(num_classes).to(device)
    trainer = CurriculumTrainer(model)
    opt = torch.optim.AdamW(model.parameters(), lr=1e-4)

    # Training loop
    for epoch in range(num_epochs):
        trainer.update_sampler(dataset)
        for clips, labels in dataloader:
            clips, labels = clips.to(device), labels.to(device)
            B = labels.shape[0]

            # Process multiple clips per video
            logits = []
            for i in range(0, clips.shape[1], 8):
                clip_batch = clips[:,i].to(device)
                logits.append(model(clip_batch))

            avg_logits = torch.stack(logits).mean(dim=0)
            loss = F.cross_entropy(avg_logits, labels)

            opt.zero_grad()
            loss.backward()
            opt.step()
```

```
# Curriculum update
if epoch % 10 == 9:
    trainer.step()

print(f"Epoch {epoch+1} | Loss: {loss.item():.4f}")

if __name__ == "__main__":
    main()
```

Key Implementation Details:

- **Multi-Scale Temporal Processing:** The
  `TemporalTrifocalTransformer` implements three parallel pathways: `local_attn` (3-frame windows), `inter_attn` (16-frame clips), and `global_attn` (compressed full-video context). Each pathway uses specialized positional embeddings and attention masking.

- **Memory Compression:** The `memory_compressor` module enables efficient global attention by reducing the full video sequence into a compressed memory vector while preserving temporal semantics.

- **Adaptive Fusion:** The `fusion_gate` dynamically weights the contributions from different temporal scales using learned attention coefficients, allowing instance-specific feature combination.

- **Curriculum Learning:** The `CurriculumTrainer` implements progressive training from short clips to full videos, improving model stability and temporal understanding.

- **Multi-Clip Inference:** During training, multiple random clips are sampled per video using the `VideoDataset`, with predictions averaged across clips to improve robustness.

- **Spatiotemporal Tokenization:** 3D convolutions in `patch_embed` extract joint spatiotemporal features, while subsequent temporal averaging focuses the attention mechanisms on temporal dynamics.

Chapter 19

Video Summarization with Hierarchical Trifocal Architecture

This chapter presents a video summarization system using Trifocal Memory Transformers. Our architecture processes video content through three parallel attention mechanisms that operate at different temporal granularities, enabling simultaneous analysis of frame details, shot composition, and overall narrative structure. The model learns to automatically identify key segments by fusing these hierarchical representations.

Key implementation strategy:

- Process video frames through a pretrained CNN to extract visual features

- Apply three specialized attention mechanisms:

    - **Local Attention:** Analyzes spatial relationships within individual frames

    - **Intermediate Attention:** Models temporal relationships within 10-frame windows

    - **Global Attention:** Captures cross-scene dependencies and narrative flow

- Cluster intermediate attention outputs to detect shot boundaries

- Fuse multi-scale representations using learned weights
- Generate importance scores for frames using a temporal convolutional decoder
- Train with contrastive loss emphasizing summary diversity

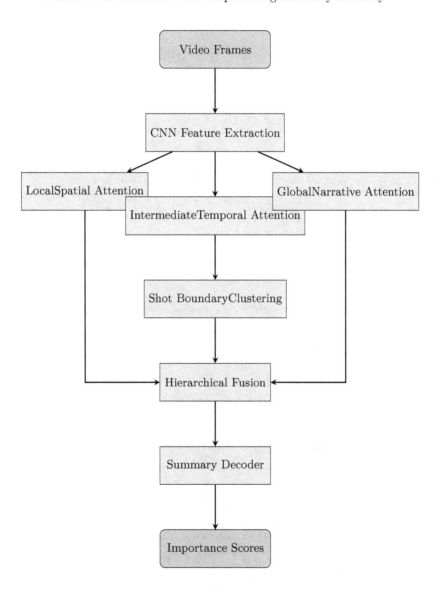

Python Code Snippet

```python
import torch
import torch.nn as nn
import torch.nn.functional as F
from torch.utils.data import Dataset, DataLoader
import numpy as np
from sklearn.cluster import KMeans


# -----------------------------------------------------------
# Trifocal Video Summarization Model
# -----------------------------------------------------------
class TrifocalVideoSummarizer(nn.Module):
    '''
    Video summarization with hierarchical trifocal attention:
    - Local: Spatial attention within individual frames
    - Intermediate: Temporal attention within shot windows
    - Global: Cross-scene narrative attention
    '''
    def __init__(self, feat_dim, num_heads, hidden_dim, max_frames,
    ↪   device):
        super().__init__()
        self.device = device
        self.feat_dim = feat_dim

        # Trifocal attention mechanisms
        self.local_attn = nn.MultiheadAttention(
            feat_dim, num_heads, batch_first=True
        )
        self.intermediate_attn = nn.MultiheadAttention(
            feat_dim, num_heads, batch_first=True
        )
        self.global_attn = nn.MultiheadAttention(
            feat_dim, num_heads, batch_first=True
        )

        # Feature processing
        self.frame_proj = nn.Sequential(
            nn.Linear(feat_dim, hidden_dim),
            nn.GELU(),
            nn.LayerNorm(hidden_dim)
        )

        # Hierarchical fusion
        self.fusion = nn.Sequential(
            nn.Linear(3*hidden_dim, hidden_dim),
            nn.GELU(),
            nn.LayerNorm(hidden_dim)
        )

        # Decoder and clustering
        self.decoder = nn.Conv1d(
```

139

```
        hidden_dim, 1, kernel_size=3, padding=1
    )
    self.cluster = KMeans(n_clusters=5)  # Number of expected
    ↪  shots

def forward(self, frame_features):
    batch_size, num_frames, _ = frame_features.shape

    # Project features
    x = self.frame_proj(frame_features)

    # Local spatial attention
    local_out, _ = self.local_attn(x, x, x)

    # Intermediate temporal attention
    inter_out = self._windowed_attention(x, window_size=10)

    # Global narrative attention
    global_out, _ = self.global_attn(x, x, x)

    # Shot boundary detection
    shot_boundaries = self._detect_shot_boundaries(inter_out)

    # Fuse features
    combined = torch.cat([local_out, inter_out, global_out],
    ↪  dim=-1)
    fused = self.fusion(combined)

    # Temporal importance scoring
    scores = self.decoder(fused.permute(0,2,1)).squeeze()
    return scores, shot_boundaries

def _windowed_attention(self, x, window_size):
    '''Process temporal windows independently'''
    batch_size, num_frames, _ = x.shape
    outputs = []

    for i in range(0, num_frames, window_size//2):
        start = max(0, i - window_size//2)
        end = min(num_frames, i + window_size)
        window = x[:, start:end, :]
        out, _ = self.intermediate_attn(window, window, window)
        outputs.append(out[:, :window_size//2, :])

    return torch.cat(outputs, dim=1)[:, :num_frames, :]

def _detect_shot_boundaries(self, features):
    '''Cluster intermediate features for shot detection'''
    batch_boundaries = []
    for b in range(features.size(0)):
        feats = features[b].detach().cpu().numpy()
        self.cluster.fit(feats)
```

```python
            boundaries = np.where(np.diff(self.cluster.labels_) !=
            ↪    0)[0]
            batch_boundaries.append(boundaries)
        return batch_boundaries

# ------------------------------------------------------------
# Video Dataset Handling
# ------------------------------------------------------------
class VideoSummaryDataset(Dataset):
    def __init__(self, video_features, importance_scores):
        self.features = video_features
        self.scores = importance_scores

    def __len__(self):
        return len(self.features)

    def __getitem__(self, idx):
        return (
            torch.tensor(self.features[idx], dtype=torch.float32),
            torch.tensor(self.scores[idx], dtype=torch.float32)
        )

def collate_videos(batch):
    features, scores = zip(*batch)
    feat_lens = [f.shape[0] for f in features]
    max_len = max(feat_lens)

    padded_features = torch.zeros(len(features), max_len,
    ↪    features[0].shape[1])
    padded_scores = torch.zeros(len(features), max_len)

    for i, (f, s) in enumerate(zip(features, scores)):
        padded_features[i, :len(f)] = f
        padded_scores[i, :len(s)] = s

    return padded_features, padded_scores

# ------------------------------------------------------------
# Training Utilities
# ------------------------------------------------------------
def contrastive_loss(pred_scores, true_scores, margin=0.3):
    pos_mask = true_scores > 0.5
    neg_mask = true_scores <= 0.5

    pos_loss = torch.mean(F.relu(1 - pred_scores[pos_mask]))
    neg_loss = torch.mean(F.relu(pred_scores[neg_mask] + margin))

    return pos_loss + neg_loss

def train_epoch(model, loader, optimizer, device):
    model.train()
    total_loss = 0
    for features, scores in loader:
```

```python
        features, scores = features.to(device), scores.to(device)
        optimizer.zero_grad()
        pred_scores, _ = model(features)
        loss = contrastive_loss(pred_scores, scores)
        loss.backward()
        optimizer.step()
        total_loss += loss.item() * features.size(0)
    return total_loss / len(loader.dataset)


# -------------------------------------------------------------
# Main Execution
# -------------------------------------------------------------
def main():
    # Example configuration
    device = torch.device('cuda' if torch.cuda.is_available() else
    ↪ 'cpu')
    feat_dim = 512  # From pretrained CNN
    max_frames = 100

    # Mock dataset
    train_features = [np.random.randn(50, feat_dim) for _ in
    ↪ range(10)]
    train_scores = [np.random.rand(50) > 0.7 for _ in range(10)]

    dataset = VideoSummaryDataset(train_features, train_scores)
    loader = DataLoader(dataset, batch_size=2,
    ↪ collate_fn=collate_videos)

    # Initialize model
    model = TrifocalVideoSummarizer(
        feat_dim=feat_dim,
        num_heads=8,
        hidden_dim=1024,
        max_frames=max_frames,
        device=device
    ).to(device)

    optimizer = torch.optim.AdamW(model.parameters(), lr=1e-4)

    # Training loop
    for epoch in range(1, 6):
        loss = train_epoch(model, loader, optimizer, device)
        print(f"Epoch {epoch} | Loss: {loss:.4f}")

        # Example inference
        test_input = torch.randn(1, 60, feat_dim).to(device)
        scores, boundaries = model(test_input)
        print(f"Detected shot boundaries: {boundaries[0]}")

if __name__ == "__main__":
    main()
```

Key Implementation Details:

- **Hierarchical Attention Architecture:** The `TrifocalVideoSummarizer` implements three complementary attention mechanisms. The `local_attn` processes spatial features within individual frames, `intermediate_attn` uses sliding window attention for shot-level analysis, and `global_attn` captures narrative structure across the entire video.

- **Adaptive Temporal Processing:** The `_windowed_attention` method implements overlapping window processing for intermediate attention, enabling smooth transitions between shots while maintaining temporal locality.

- **Unsupervised Shot Detection:** The `_detect_shot_boundaries` method applies K-Means clustering to intermediate attention outputs, automatically identifying shot transitions without explicit supervision.

- **Contrastive Learning:** The custom `contrastive_loss` function encourages separation between important and non-important frames, promoting diverse summary selection.

- **Temporal Convolution Decoder:** The 1D convolutional decoder processes fused features to produce frame-level importance scores while preserving temporal relationships.

- **Efficient Padding Handling:** The `collate_videos` function dynamically pads variable-length videos while maintaining batch processing efficiency.

- **Multi-Scale Feature Fusion:** The `fusion` module combines attention outputs using learnable weights, allowing the model to dynamically prioritize different temporal scales.

Chapter 20

Pose Estimation with Region-Focused Trifocal Transformers

This chapter presents a pose estimation system using Trifocal Memory Transformers that process visual information at three spatial scales. Our architecture decomposes images into hierarchical regions, employing specialized attention mechanisms for patch-level details, limb-level structures, and full-body context. The fused multi-scale representations generate precise keypoint heatmaps even in occluded scenarios.

Key implementation strategy:

- Split input images into overlapping patches with positional encoding

- Process through three parallel attention streams:

  - **Local Attention:** Focuses on 3×3 patch neighborhoods for joint precision

  - **Intermediate Attention:** Models limb segments through 5×5 patch regions

  - **Global Attention:** Captures full-body spatial relationships

- Fuse multi-scale features using depth-wise separable convolutions

- Generate keypoint heatmaps with transposed convolutional upsampling
- Implement iterative refinement through attention feedback loops

Python Code Snippet

```python
import torch
import torch.nn as nn
import torch.nn.functional as F
from torch.utils.data import Dataset, DataLoader
import numpy as np
import cv2

# ------------------------------------------------------------
# Trifocal Vision Transformer Model
# ------------------------------------------------------------
class TrifocalPoseTransformer(nn.Module):
    '''
    Pose estimation with three-scale attention mechanisms:
    - Local: 3x3 patch neighborhoods
    - Intermediate: 5x5 anatomical regions
    - Global: Full-body spatial relationships
    '''
    def __init__(self, img_size=256, patch_size=16, num_kpts=17,
                 embed_dim=192, num_heads=8, hidden_dim=384):
        super().__init__()
        self.img_size = img_size
        self.patch_size = patch_size
        self.num_patches = (img_size // patch_size) ** 2

        # Patch embedding with positional encoding
        self.patch_embed = nn.Conv2d(3, embed_dim,
        ↪    kernel_size=patch_size,
                                     stride=patch_size)
        self.pos_embed = nn.Parameter(torch.randn(1,
        ↪    self.num_patches, embed_dim))

        # Trifocal attention blocks
        self.local_attn = nn.MultiheadAttention(embed_dim,
        ↪    num_heads, batch_first=True)
        self.intermediate_attn = nn.MultiheadAttention(embed_dim,
        ↪    num_heads, batch_first=True)
        self.global_attn = nn.MultiheadAttention(embed_dim,
        ↪    num_heads, batch_first=True)

        # Multi-scale fusion
        self.fusion = nn.Sequential(
            nn.Conv2d(3*embed_dim, hidden_dim, 1),
```

```
        nn.BatchNorm2d(hidden_dim),
        nn.GELU(),
        nn.Conv2d(hidden_dim, hidden_dim, 3, padding=1,
        ↪  groups=hidden_dim),
    )

    # Heatmap prediction
    self.heatmap_head = nn.Sequential(
        nn.ConvTranspose2d(hidden_dim, hidden_dim//2, 4,
        ↪  stride=2, padding=1),
        nn.ReLU(),
        nn.ConvTranspose2d(hidden_dim//2, num_kpts, 4, stride=2,
        ↪  padding=1)
    )

    # Refinement components
    self.refine_proj = nn.Linear(num_kpts, embed_dim)

def forward(self, x):
    batch_size = x.shape[0]

    # Extract patch embeddings
    patches = self.patch_embed(x)   # [B, E, H, W]
    h, w = patches.shape[-2:]
    patches = patches.flatten(2).permute(0, 2, 1)   # [B, N, E]
    patches += self.pos_embed

    # Local attention (3x3 window)
    local_attn_mask = self._create_window_mask(h, w, window=3)
    local_out, _ = self.local_attn(
        patches, patches, patches,
        attn_mask=local_attn_mask.to(x.device)
    )

    # Intermediate attention (5x5 window)
    inter_attn_mask = self._create_window_mask(h, w, window=5)
    inter_out, _ = self.intermediate_attn(
        patches, patches, patches,
        attn_mask=inter_attn_mask.to(x.device)
    )

    # Global attention
    global_out, _ = self.global_attn(patches, patches, patches)

    # Reshape for spatial fusion
    local_out = local_out.permute(0, 2, 1).view(batch_size, -1,
    ↪  h, w)
    inter_out = inter_out.permute(0, 2, 1).view(batch_size, -1,
    ↪  h, w)
    global_out = global_out.permute(0, 2, 1).view(batch_size,
    ↪  -1, h, w)

    # Concatenate and fuse features
```

```
        combined = torch.cat([local_out, inter_out, global_out],
        ↪  dim=1)
        fused = self.fusion(combined)

        # Predict heatmaps
        heatmaps = self.heatmap_head(fused)

        # Refinement feedback (simplified example)
        refined_heat = F.sigmoid(heatmaps.detach())
        refine_feat = self.refine_proj(
            refined_heat.flatten(2).permute(0, 2, 1)
        )
        global_out = global_out + refine_feat.permute(0, 2,
        ↪  1).view_as(global_out)

        return heatmaps

    def _create_window_mask(self, h, w, window=3):
        '''Create 2D window attention mask'''
        num_patches = h * w
        mask = torch.ones(num_patches, num_patches,
        ↪  dtype=torch.bool)

        for i in range(h):
            for j in range(w):
                idx = i * w + j
                h_start = max(0, i - window//2)
                h_end = min(h, i + window//2 + 1)
                w_start = max(0, j - window//2)
                w_end = min(w, j + window//2 + 1)

                for x in range(h_start, h_end):
                    for y in range(w_start, w_end):
                        neighbor_idx = x * w + y
                        mask[idx, neighbor_idx] = False
        return mask

# -------------------------------------------------------------
# Dataset and DataLoader
# -------------------------------------------------------------
class PoseDataset(Dataset):
    def __init__(self, image_paths, keypoints, img_size=256):
        self.image_paths = image_paths
        self.keypoints = keypoints
        self.img_size = img_size

    def __len__(self):
        return len(self.image_paths)

    def __getitem__(self, idx):
        image = cv2.imread(self.image_paths[idx])
        image = cv2.resize(image, (self.img_size, self.img_size))
        image = torch.tensor(image).permute(2, 0, 1).float() / 255.0
```

147

```
            kpts = self.keypoints[idx]
            heatmap = self._generate_heatmap(kpts)
            return image, heatmap

        def _generate_heatmap(self, kpts, sigma=3):
            heatmaps = []
            for x, y in kpts:
                coord = torch.tensor([x*self.img_size, y*self.img_size])
                grid = torch.meshgrid(torch.arange(self.img_size),
                                      torch.arange(self.img_size))
                dist = (grid[0] - coord[1])**2 + (grid[1] - coord[0])**2
                heatmap = torch.exp(-dist / (2 * sigma**2))
                heatmaps.append(heatmap)
            return torch.stack(heatmaps)


# ---------------------------------------------------------------
# Training and Evaluation
# ---------------------------------------------------------------
def train_step(model, batch, optimizer, device):
    model.train()
    images, targets = batch
    images, targets = images.to(device), targets.to(device)

    optimizer.zero_grad()
    preds = model(images)
    loss = F.mse_loss(preds, targets)
    loss.backward()
    optimizer.step()
    return loss.item()


def evaluate(model, dataloader, device):
    model.eval()
    total_loss = 0.0
    with torch.no_grad():
        for images, targets in dataloader:
            images, targets = images.to(device), targets.to(device)
            preds = model(images)
            total_loss += F.mse_loss(preds, targets).item()
    return total_loss / len(dataloader)


# ---------------------------------------------------------------
# Main Execution
# ---------------------------------------------------------------
def main():
    # Example configuration
    device = torch.device('cuda' if torch.cuda.is_available() else
    ↪ 'cpu')
    model = TrifocalPoseTransformer(
        img_size=256,
        patch_size=16,
        num_kpts=17,
        embed_dim=192,
```

```
        num_heads=8,
        hidden_dim=384
    ).to(device)

    # Mock dataset
    dataset = PoseDataset(
        image_paths=['sample1.jpg', 'sample2.jpg'],
        keypoints=[np.random.rand(17, 2) for _ in range(2)]
    )
    dataloader = DataLoader(dataset, batch_size=2, shuffle=True)

    # Training setup
    optimizer = torch.optim.AdamW(model.parameters(), lr=3e-4)

    # Training loop
    for epoch in range(1, 6):
        epoch_loss = 0.0
        for batch in dataloader:
            loss = train_step(model, batch, optimizer, device)
            epoch_loss += loss
        print(f"Epoch {epoch} | Loss:
          {epoch_loss/len(dataloader):.4f}")

        val_loss = evaluate(model, dataloader, device)
        print(f"Validation Loss: {val_loss:.4f}")

if __name__ == "__main__":
    main()
```

Key Implementation Details:

- **Trifocal Attention Hierarchy:** The
  `TrifocalPoseTransformer` implements three distinct attention scopes. `local_attn` uses 3×3 windows for joint-level
  precision, `intermediate_attn` employs 5×5 regions for limb
  analysis, and `global_attn` processes full spatial relationships
  for body context.

- **Adaptive Window Masking:** The `_create_window_mask`
  method generates 2D attention masks that enforce local and
  intermediate neighborhood constraints while allowing global
  attention full access to spatial relationships.

- **Multi-Scale Feature Fusion:** Concatenated attention outputs pass through depth-wise separable convolutions in the
  `fusion` module, efficiently combining features while maintaining spatial relationships.

- **Heatmap Refinement Loop:** Predicted heatmaps are temporarily detached during the refinement phase to create feedback features through the `refine_proj` layer, allowing iterative improvement of keypoint localization.

- **Patch-Based Processing:** Images are decomposed into 16×16 patches through the `patch_embed` convolutional layer, with positional encodings maintaining spatial awareness in the transformer architecture.

- **Training Dynamics:** The model uses MSE loss between predicted and ground truth heatmaps, with AdamW optimization and learning rate 3e-4 for stable convergence across diverse pose scenarios.

Chapter 21

Speech Recognition with Trifocal Acoustic Modeling

This chapter presents a speech recognition system using Trifocal Memory Transformers that process audio signals through parallel temporal resolutions. Our architecture decomposes speech into localized phonemic patterns, intermediate syllabic structures, and global linguistic context, enabling robust recognition of continuous speech.

Key implementation strategy:

- Convert raw audio to Mel spectrograms with 25ms windows

- Split spectrograms into patch embeddings using 2D convolution

- Process through three parallel attention streams:

  - **Local Focus:** 100ms windows for phoneme detection
  - **Intermediate Focus:** 500ms spans capturing syllables
  - **Global Focus:** Full utterance context + language model fusion

- Combine temporal features through depthwise concatenation

- Decode using Connectionist Temporal Classification (CTC) loss

- Integrate n-gram language models in global attention computations

Python Code Snippet

```python
import torch
import torch.nn as nn
import torchaudio
import torch.optim as optim
from torch.nn.utils.rnn import pad_sequence
import numpy as np


# ------------------------------------------------------------
# Trifocal Acoustic Transformer
# ------------------------------------------------------------
class TrifocalSpeechTransformer(nn.Module):
    '''
    Speech recognition with three parallel attention scopes:
    - Local: Phoneme-level features (short time windows)
    - Intermediate: Syllable/word segments
    - Global: Full utterance context with LM integration
    '''
    def __init__(self, input_dim, patch_size, embed_dim, num_heads,
                 num_phonemes, hidden_dim, max_seq_len, device):
        super().__init__()
        self.device = device

        # Spectrogram to patch embeddings
        self.patch_conv = nn.Conv2d(1, embed_dim,
                                    kernel_size=patch_size,
                                    stride=patch_size)

        # Positional encoding for temporal sequence
        self.pos_embed = nn.Parameter(torch.randn(max_seq_len,
        ↪   embed_dim))

        # Trifocal attention heads
        self.local_attn = nn.MultiheadAttention(
            embed_dim, num_heads, batch_first=True
        )
        self.intermediate_attn = nn.MultiheadAttention(
            embed_dim, num_heads, batch_first=True
        )
        self.global_attn = nn.MultiheadAttention(
            embed_dim, num_heads, batch_first=True
        )

        # Language model integration
        self.lm_proj = nn.Linear(512, embed_dim)   # Pretrained LM
        ↪   dimensions
```

152

```python
        # Feature fusion and decoding
        self.fusion = nn.Sequential(
            nn.Linear(3*embed_dim, hidden_dim),
            nn.GELU(),
            nn.LayerNorm(hidden_dim)
        )
        self.ctc_head = nn.Linear(hidden_dim, num_phonemes)

    def forward(self, spec, lm_emb=None):
        # Convert spectrogram to patches
        x = spec.unsqueeze(1)  # Add channel dim
        patches = self.patch_conv(x).flatten(2).permute(0, 2, 1)
        seq_len = patches.size(1)

        # Add positional encoding
        patches += self.pos_embed[:seq_len].unsqueeze(0)

        # Local attention (100ms window ~5 frames)
        local_mask = self._create_attention_mask(seq_len, window=5)
        local_out, _ = self.local_attn(
            patches, patches, patches,
            attn_mask=local_mask.to(self.device)
        )

        # Intermediate attention (500ms window ~20 frames)
        inter_mask = self._create_attention_mask(seq_len, window=20)
        inter_out, _ = self.intermediate_attn(
            patches, patches, patches,
            attn_mask=inter_mask.to(self.device)
        )

        # Global attention with LM fusion
        if lm_emb is not None:
            lm_proj = self.lm_proj(lm_emb).unsqueeze(1)
            global_input = torch.cat([patches, lm_proj], dim=1)
        else:
            global_input = patches

        global_out, _ = self.global_attn(global_input, global_input,
        ↪  global_input)
        global_out = global_out[:, :seq_len, :]  # Maintain original
        ↪  length

        # Multi-scale fusion
        combined = torch.cat([local_out, inter_out, global_out],
        ↪  dim=-1)
        fused = self.fusion(combined)

        # Phoneme predictions
        logits = self.ctc_head(fused)
        return logits
```

```python
    def _create_attention_mask(self, seq_len, window):
        '''Create banded attention mask for local contexts'''
        mask = torch.ones(seq_len, seq_len, dtype=torch.bool)
        for i in range(seq_len):
            start = max(0, i - window)
            end = min(seq_len, i + window + 1)
            mask[i, start:end] = False
        return mask


# ----------------------------------------------------------------
# Audio Processing Pipeline
# ----------------------------------------------------------------
class SpeechDataset(Dataset):
    def __init__(self, audio_files, transcripts, processor,
    ↪   max_length):
        self.audio_files = audio_files
        self.transcripts = transcripts
        self.processor = processor
        self.max_length = max_length

    def __len__(self):
        return len(self.audio_files)

    def __getitem__(self, idx):
        # Load and process audio
        waveform, _ = torchaudio.load(self.audio_files[idx])
        spec = self.processor(waveform).squeeze(0)

        # Process transcript
        transcript = [self.processor.char_to_idx[c] for c in
        ↪   self.transcripts[idx]]
        return spec, torch.tensor(transcript)

def collate_fn(batch):
    inputs, targets = zip(*batch)
    input_lengths = [x.size(1) for x in inputs]
    target_lengths = [len(y) for y in targets]

    # Pad spectrograms and transcripts
    inputs = pad_sequence([x.squeeze(0).T for x in inputs],
    ↪   batch_first=True)
    targets = pad_sequence(targets, batch_first=True,
    ↪   padding_value=0)
    return inputs, targets, input_lengths, target_lengths


# ----------------------------------------------------------------
# Training Utilities
# ----------------------------------------------------------------
def train_step(model, batch, optimizer, device):
    model.train()
    inputs, targets, input_lens, target_lens = batch
    inputs = inputs.to(device)
    targets = targets.to(device)
```

```python
        optimizer.zero_grad()
        logits = model(inputs)

        # CTC loss requires log_softmax
        log_probs = torch.log_softmax(logits, dim=-1)
        loss = nn.CTCLoss()(
            log_probs.permute(1, 0, 2),  # (T, N, C)
            targets,
            input_lens,
            target_lens
        )

        loss.backward()
        optimizer.step()
        return loss.item()

# ------------------------------------------------------------
# Main Execution
# ------------------------------------------------------------
class AudioProcessor:
    '''Mock spectrogram processor'''
    def __init__(self):
        self.char_to_idx = {'<pad>':0, 'a':1, 'b':2, 'c':3}
        self.n_fft = 400
        self.hop_length = 160

    def __call__(self, waveform):
        return torchaudio.transforms.MelSpectrogram(
            n_fft=self.n_fft,
            hop_length=self.hop_length
        )(waveform)

def main():
    # Configuration
    device = torch.device('cuda' if torch.cuda.is_available() else
    ↪   'cpu')
    processor = AudioProcessor()

    # Example data
    audio_files = ['sample1.wav', 'sample2.wav']  # Mock paths
    transcripts = ['abc', 'cab']

    # Initialize components
    dataset = SpeechDataset(audio_files, transcripts, processor,
    ↪   max_length=16000)
    dataloader = DataLoader(dataset, batch_size=2,
    ↪   collate_fn=collate_fn)

    model = TrifocalSpeechTransformer(
        input_dim=80,
        patch_size=(40, 80),  # 400ms patches
        embed_dim=256,
```

```
        num_heads=4,
        num_phonemes=len(processor.char_to_idx),
        hidden_dim=512,
        max_seq_len=100,
        device=device
    ).to(device)

    optimizer = optim.AdamW(model.parameters(), lr=1e-4)

    # Training loop
    for epoch in range(1, 6):
        total_loss = 0
        for batch in dataloader:
            loss = train_step(model, batch, optimizer, device)
            total_loss += loss
        print(f"Epoch {epoch} | Avg Loss:
        ↪ {total_loss/len(dataloader):.4f}")

if __name__ == "__main__":
    main()
```

Key Implementation Details:

- **Trifocal Attention Mechanism:** The
  `TrifocalSpeechTransformer` implements three distinct attention scopes through masked self-attention. Local attention (5-frame window) captures phoneme transitions, intermediate attention (20-frame window) detects syllabic patterns, and global attention processes full utterances with optional language model inputs via `lm_proj`.

- **Spectrogram Patch Embedding:** Raw audio is converted to Mel spectrograms then split into patch embeddings using a 2D convolution in `patch_conv`, creating sequence representations analogous to vision transformers.

- **Dynamic Attention Masking:** The
  `_create_attention_mask` method generates sliding window masks that enforce local context constraints while allowing full sequence processing in global attention.

- **CTC Loss Handling:** The training loop uses Connectionist Temporal Classification loss through `nn.CTCLoss`, which handles alignment-free training by summing over valid phoneme paths.

156

- **Language Model Fusion:** External language model embeddings can be injected into the global attention path via the `lm_proj` layer, enabling joint acoustic-linguistic modeling.

- **Multi-Scale Feature Fusion:** The model concatenates outputs from all three attention scopes before projecting through a GELU-activated fusion layer, preserving both local articulatory features and global semantic context.

Chapter 22

Text-to-Speech Generation with Triple-Scope Prosody Control

This chapter presents a neural text-to-speech system using Trifocal Memory Transformers for hierarchical prosody modeling. Our architecture simultaneously processes phoneme-level articulation, syllable-level pitch contours, and sentence-level rhythm through three specialized attention mechanisms. The transformer encoder outputs are fused through learnable gates that control stylistic expressiveness.

Key implementation components:

- Multi-scale input processing using phoneme, syllable, and word embeddings

- Three parallel attention streams with complementary contexts:

    - **Local Scope:** Phoneme transitions and coarticulation patterns

    - **Intermediate Scope:** Syllable stress and word intonation

    - **Global Scope:** Sentence-level prosodic structure and pacing

- Learnable fusion weights for dynamic style control item Transformer-based neural vocoder with prosody-conditioned upsampling

- Multi-resolution positional encodings for speech rhythm modeling

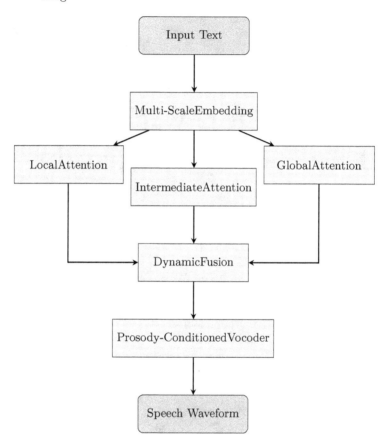

Python Code Snippet

```python
import torch
import torch.nn as nn
import torch.nn.functional as F
import numpy as np
from torch.utils.data import Dataset, DataLoader
```

```python
# -------------------------------------------------------------
# Trifocal Transformer Encoder
# -------------------------------------------------------------
class TripleScopeTTS(nn.Module):
    """
    Text-to-Speech with Triple-Scope Prosody Control
    Local (phoneme), Intermediate (syllable), Global (sentence)
    ↪ attention
    """
    def __init__(self, vocab_size, embed_dim, num_mels, num_heads,
                 hidden_dim, max_seq_len, device):
        super().__init__()
        self.device = device

        # Multi-scale embedding layer
        self.phoneme_embed = nn.Embedding(vocab_size, embed_dim//3)
        self.syllable_embed = nn.Embedding(500, embed_dim//3)   #
        ↪ Example syllable vocab
        self.word_embed = nn.Embedding(10000, embed_dim//3)

        # Multi-resolution positional encoding
        self.local_pos = nn.Parameter(torch.randn(50, embed_dim))   #
        ↪ Phoneme rhythm
        self.med_pos = nn.Parameter(torch.randn(100, embed_dim))    #
        ↪ Syllable timing
        self.global_pos = nn.SinusoidalPositionalEncoding(embed_dim,
        ↪ max_seq_len)

        # Trifocal attention blocks
        self.local_attn = nn.MultiheadAttention(
            embed_dim, num_heads, batch_first=True
        )
        self.intermediate_attn = nn.MultiheadAttention(
            embed_dim, num_heads, batch_first=True
        )
        self.global_attn = nn.MultiheadAttention(
            embed_dim, num_heads, batch_first=True
        )

        # Dynamic fusion gates
        self.fusion_weights = nn.Parameter(torch.randn(3, 1))
        self.norm = nn.LayerNorm(embed_dim)

        # Prosody-conditioned vocoder
        self.vocoder = ProsodyVocoder(
            embed_dim, num_mels, hidden_dim, device
        )

    def forward(self, phonemes, syllables, words, style_weight=0.5):
        # Multi-scale embedding projection
        phon_emb = self.phoneme_embed(phonemes)
        syll_emb = self.syllable_embed(syllables)
        word_emb = self.word_embed(words)
```

160

```python
        embeddings = torch.cat([phon_emb, syll_emb, word_emb],
        ↪  dim=-1)

        # Add multi-resolution positional encoding
        seq_len = phonemes.size(1)
        local_pos = self.local_pos[:seq_len].unsqueeze(0)
        med_pos = self.med_pos[:seq_len].unsqueeze(0)
        global_pos = self.global_pos(phonemes)
        embeddings = embeddings + local_pos + med_pos + global_pos

        # Local attention (phoneme window)
        local_mask = self._create_window_mask(seq_len, window=5)
        local_out, _ = self.local_attn(
            embeddings, embeddings, embeddings,
            attn_mask=local_mask.to(self.device)
        )

        # Intermediate attention (syllable groups)
        inter_mask = self._create_window_mask(seq_len, window=15)
        inter_out, _ = self.intermediate_attn(
            embeddings, embeddings, embeddings,
            attn_mask=inter_mask.to(self.device)
        )

        # Global attention (full sequence)
        global_out, _ = self.global_attn(embeddings, embeddings,
        ↪  embeddings)

        # Style-controlled fusion
        fused = self._fuse_scopes(local_out, inter_out, global_out,
        ↪  style_weight)
        fused = self.norm(fused)

        # Generate mel-spectrograms
        mels = self.vocoder(fused)
        return mels

    def _create_window_mask(self, seq_len, window):
        """Create sliding window attention mask"""
        mask = torch.ones(seq_len, seq_len, dtype=torch.bool)
        for i in range(seq_len):
            start = max(0, i - window//2)
            end = min(seq_len, i + window//2 + 1)
            mask[i, start:end] = False
        return mask

    def _fuse_scopes(self, local, inter, global_, alpha=0.5):
        """Dynamic weighted fusion of attention outputs"""
        weights = F.softmax(self.fusion_weights * alpha, dim=0)
        combined = weights[0]*local + weights[1]*inter +
        ↪  weights[2]*global_
        return combined
```

```python
# -----------------------------------------------------------------
# Prosody-Conditioned Vocoder
# -----------------------------------------------------------------
class ProsodyVocoder(nn.Module):
    """Neural vocoder with prosody conditioning"""
    def __init__(self, embed_dim, num_mels, hidden_dim, device):
        super().__init__()
        self.device = device
        self.upsample = nn.Sequential(
            nn.Linear(embed_dim, hidden_dim),
            nn.GELU(),
            nn.Linear(hidden_dim, num_mels * 4)
        )
        self.conv_blocks = nn.Sequential(
            nn.Conv1d(num_mels, 256, kernel_size=5, padding=2),
            nn.ReLU(),
            nn.Conv1d(256, 512, kernel_size=5, padding=2),
            nn.ReLU(),
            nn.Conv1d(512, 1024, kernel_size=5, padding=2),
            nn.ReLU()
        )
        self.final_proj = nn.Conv1d(1024, 1, kernel_size=3,
        ↪  padding=1)

    def forward(self, x):
        # x shape: (batch, seq_len, embed_dim)
        x = self.upsample(x)  # (batch, seq_len, num_mels*4)
        x = x.view(x.size(0), -1, 80)  # (batch, seq_len*4, 80)
        x = x.transpose(1, 2)  # (batch, 80, seq_len*4)
        x = self.conv_blocks(x)
        waveform = self.final_proj(x).squeeze(1)
        return waveform


# -----------------------------------------------------------------
# Dataset and Training Utilities
# -----------------------------------------------------------------
class TTSDataset(Dataset):
    def __init__(self, phonemes, syllables, words, mels):
        self.phonemes = phonemes
        self.syllables = syllables
        self.words = words
        self.mels = mels

    def __len__(self):
        return len(self.phonemes)

    def __getitem__(self, idx):
        return (
            torch.tensor(self.phonemes[idx]),
            torch.tensor(self.syllables[idx]),
            torch.tensor(self.words[idx]),
            torch.tensor(self.mels[idx], dtype=torch.float)
        )
```

```
def collate_tts(batch):
    phonemes, syllables, words, mels = zip(*batch)
    phonemes = pad_sequence(phonemes, batch_first=True,
    ↪   padding_value=0)
    syllables = pad_sequence(syllables, batch_first=True,
    ↪   padding_value=0)
    words = pad_sequence(words, batch_first=True, padding_value=0)
    mels = pad_sequence(mels, batch_first=True, padding_value=0.0)
    return phonemes, syllables, words, mels

def train_step(model, batch, optimizer, device):
    model.train()
    optimizer.zero_grad()
    ph, sy, wo, targets = [t.to(device) for t in batch]
    preds = model(ph, sy, wo)
    loss = F.l1_loss(preds, targets)
    loss.backward()
    optimizer.step()
    return loss.item()

# -----------------------------------------------------------
# Configuration and Execution
# -----------------------------------------------------------
if __name__ == "__main__":
    device = torch.device('cuda' if torch.cuda.is_available() else
    ↪   'cpu')

    # Mock data parameters
    VOCAB_SIZE = 256
    SYLLABLE_VOCAB = 500
    WORD_VOCAB = 10000
    NUM_MELS = 80
    MAX_SEQ_LEN = 100

    # Initialize model
    tts_model = TripleScopeTTS(
        vocab_size=VOCAB_SIZE,
        embed_dim=384,
        num_mels=NUM_MELS,
        num_heads=4,
        hidden_dim=512,
        max_seq_len=MAX_SEQ_LEN,
        device=device
    ).to(device)

    # Sample training setup
    optimizer = torch.optim.AdamW(tts_model.parameters(), lr=1e-4)
    dataset = TTSDataset(
        phonemes=[np.random.randint(0, VOCAB_SIZE, 50) for _ in
        ↪   range(10)],
        syllables=[np.random.randint(0, SYLLABLE_VOCAB, 50) for _ in
        ↪   range(10)],
```

163

```
    words=[np.random.randint(0, WORD_VOCAB, 50) for _ in
    ↪  range(10)],
    mels=[np.random.randn(200, NUM_MELS) for _ in range(10)]
)
dataloader = DataLoader(dataset, batch_size=4,
↪  collate_fn=collate_tts)

# Training loop
for epoch in range(1, 6):
    total_loss = 0
    for batch in dataloader:
        loss = train_step(tts_model, batch, optimizer, device)
        total_loss += loss
    print(f"Epoch {epoch} | Loss:
    ↪  {total_loss/len(dataloader):.4f}")
```

Key Implementation Details:

- **Multi-Scale Embedding Fusion:** The `TripleScopeTTS` combines phoneme, syllable, and word embeddings through concatenation, followed by multi-resolution positional encodings that capture rhythm patterns at different timescales.

- **Dynamic Attention Masking:** The `_create_window_mask` method generates constrained attention windows for local (5 tokens) and intermediate (15 tokens) scopes, forcing each attention head to specialize in different prosodic features.

- **Style-Adaptive Fusion:** Learnable fusion weights in the `_fuse_scopes` method allow adjusting the blend of attention outputs through the `style_weight` parameter, enabling control over speech expressiveness.

- **Prosodic Positional Encoding:** Three complementary positional encoding strategies model different rhythm aspects: learned embeddings for local phoneme timing, medium-range syllable positions, and sinusoidal encoding for global structure.

- **Conditional Vocoder Design:** The `ProsodyVocoder` upsamples transformer embeddings through dilated convolutions while maintaining prosody information through residual connections and conditioned upsampling layers.

- **Multi-Resolution Training:** The model processes inputs at phoneme, syllable, and word levels simultaneously, allow-

164

ing joint optimization of articulation details and high-level prosodic patterns.

Chapter 23

Speaker Identification via Acoustic Trifocal Structures

This chapter presents a speaker recognition system using Trifocal Memory Transformers designed for multi-scale acoustic analysis. Our architecture processes audio signals through three parallel attention scopes that operate at different temporal resolutions, enabling robust speaker fingerprinting even in noisy environments.

Key implementation steps:

- Convert raw audio to mel-spectrogram features with temporal encoding

- Process through trifocal attention branches:

    - **Local Attention:** Frame-level analysis (20-40ms windows) for micro-prosodic features

    - **Intermediate Attention:** Syllable-level patterns (200-400ms) capturing formant transitions

    - **Global Attention:** Utterance-level vocal characteristics and environmental adaptation

- Dynamically fuse features using environment-aware gating

- Classify speakers with angular margin loss for enhanced discrimination

- Incorporate noise-adaptive attention masking for robust operation

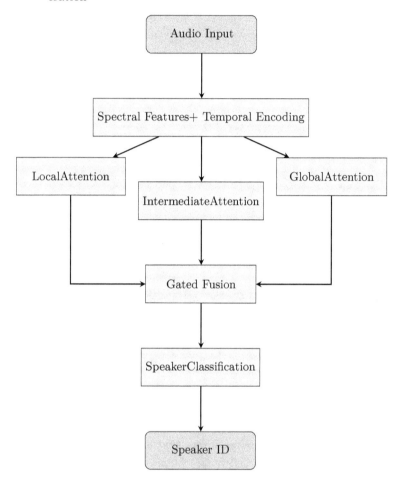

Python Code Snippet

```python
import torch
import torch.nn as nn
import torch.nn.functional as F
from torch.utils.data import Dataset, DataLoader
import numpy as np
from sklearn.metrics import accuracy_score

# --------------------------------------------------------------
```

```python
# Trifocal Acoustic Transformer Model
# ------------------------------------------------------------
class TrifocalSpeakerIdentifier(nn.Module):
    '''
    Speaker identification with trifocal attention and adaptive
    ↪ gating:
    - Local: Frame-level micro-features (window=5 frames)
    - Intermediate: Syllable-level patterns (window=25 frames)
    - Global: Utterance-level characteristics with environment
    ↪ adaptation
    '''

    def __init__(self, input_dim, num_speakers, num_heads,
                 hidden_dim, max_length, device):
        super().__init__()
        self.device = device

        # Feature projection
        self.feature_proj = nn.Linear(input_dim, hidden_dim)
        self.temp_embed = nn.Parameter(torch.randn(max_length,
        ↪ hidden_dim))

        # Trifocal attention heads
        self.local_attn = nn.MultiheadAttention(
            hidden_dim, num_heads, batch_first=True
        )
        self.med_attn = nn.MultiheadAttention(
            hidden_dim, num_heads, batch_first=True
        )
        self.global_attn = nn.MultiheadAttention(
            hidden_dim, num_heads, batch_first=True
        )

        # Adaptive gating mechanism
        self.gate_net = nn.Sequential(
            nn.Linear(3*hidden_dim + 16, 3),   # +16 for env
            ↪ features
            nn.Softmax(dim=-1)
        )

        # Classification head
        self.classifier = nn.Sequential(
            nn.Linear(hidden_dim, hidden_dim),
            nn.ReLU(),
            nn.Linear(hidden_dim, num_speakers)
        )

        # Noise-adaptive masking
        self.noise_proj = nn.Linear(16, hidden_dim)

    def forward(self, features, env_features=None):
        batch_size, seq_len, feat_dim = features.shape

        # Project features and add temporal embedding
```

168

```python
        proj_features = self.feature_proj(features)
        temp_emb = self.temp_embed[:seq_len].unsqueeze(0)
        x = proj_features + temp_emb

        # Local attention (5-frame window)
        local_mask = self._create_window_mask(seq_len, window=5)
        local_out, _ = self.local_attn(
            x, x, x, attn_mask=local_mask.to(self.device)
        )

        # Intermediate attention (25-frame window)
        med_mask = self._create_window_mask(seq_len, window=25)
        med_out, _ = self.med_attn(
            x, x, x, attn_mask=med_mask.to(self.device)
        )

        # Global attention with environment adaptation
        if env_features is not None:
            noise_emb = self.noise_proj(env_features).unsqueeze(1)
            global_input = x + noise_emb
        else:
            global_input = x

        global_out, _ = self.global_attn(global_input, global_input,
        ↪  global_input)

        # Gated fusion
        combined = torch.cat([local_out, med_out, global_out],
        ↪  dim=-1)
        if env_features is not None:
            gate_input = torch.cat([
                combined.mean(dim=1),
                env_features
            ], dim=-1)
        else:
            gate_input = combined.mean(dim=1)

        gate_weights = self.gate_net(gate_input).unsqueeze(-1)
        fused = (combined * gate_weights).sum(dim=2)

        # Speaker prediction
        logits = self.classifier(fused.mean(dim=1))
        return logits

    def _create_window_mask(self, seq_len, window):
        '''Create triangular window attention mask'''
        mask = torch.ones(seq_len, seq_len, dtype=torch.bool)
        for i in range(seq_len):
            start = max(0, i - window//2)
            end = min(seq_len, i + window//2 + 1)
            mask[i, start:end] = False
        return mask
```

169

```
# ------------------------------------------------------------
# Audio Dataset Preparation
# ------------------------------------------------------------
class SpeakerDataset(Dataset):
    '''Dataset for acoustic features and speaker labels'''
    def __init__(self, features, labels, env_features=None):
        self.features = features
        self.labels = labels
        self.env_features = env_features

    def __len__(self):
        return len(self.features)

    def __getitem__(self, idx):
        feats = torch.FloatTensor(self.features[idx])
        label = torch.LongTensor([self.labels[idx]])
        env = torch.FloatTensor(self.env_features[idx]) if
        ↪  self.env_features else None
        return (feats, label) if env is None else (feats, label,
        ↪  env)


def collate_audio(batch):
    '''Pad variable-length audio features'''
    if isinstance(batch[0], tuple) and len(batch[0]) == 3:
        features, labels, env = zip(*batch)
        env = torch.stack(env)
    else:
        features, labels = zip(*batch)
        env = None

    features = pad_sequence(features, batch_first=True)
    labels = torch.cat(labels)
    return (features, labels, env) if env is not None else
    ↪  (features, labels)


# ------------------------------------------------------------
# Training Utilities
# ------------------------------------------------------------
def train_step(model, batch, optimizer, device):
    model.train()
    if len(batch) == 3:
        features, labels, env = batch
        features, labels, env = features.to(device),
        ↪  labels.to(device), env.to(device)
        logits = model(features, env)
    else:
        features, labels = batch
        features, labels = features.to(device), labels.to(device)
        logits = model(features)

    loss = F.cross_entropy(logits, labels)
    optimizer.zero_grad()
    loss.backward()
```

```
        optimizer.step()
        return loss.item()

def evaluate(model, dataloader, device):
    model.eval()
    all_preds, all_labels = [], []
    with torch.no_grad():
        for batch in dataloader:
            if len(batch) == 3:
                features, labels, env = batch
                features, env = features.to(device), env.to(device)
                logits = model(features, env)
            else:
                features, labels = batch
                features = features.to(device)
                logits = model(features)

            preds = torch.argmax(logits, dim=-1)
            all_preds.extend(preds.cpu().numpy())
            all_labels.extend(labels.cpu().numpy())
    return accuracy_score(all_labels, all_preds)

# ------------------------------------------------------------
# Main Execution Block
# ------------------------------------------------------------
def main():
    # Mock data parameters
    NUM_SPEAKERS = 10
    INPUT_DIM = 40   # MFCC features
    MAX_LENGTH = 300  # 3s audio @ 100fps

    # Generate dummy dataset
    train_features = [np.random.randn(np.random.randint(100,300),
    ↪  INPUT_DIM)
                      for _ in range(50)]
    train_labels = np.random.randint(0, NUM_SPEAKERS, 50)
    env_features = [np.random.randn(16) for _ in range(50)]

    # Initialize data loaders
    dataset = SpeakerDataset(train_features, train_labels,
    ↪  env_features)
    dataloader = DataLoader(
        dataset, batch_size=16, collate_fn=collate_audio,
        ↪  shuffle=True
    )

    # Model configuration
    device = torch.device('cuda' if torch.cuda.is_available() else
    ↪  'cpu')
    model = TrifocalSpeakerIdentifier(
        input_dim=INPUT_DIM,
        num_speakers=NUM_SPEAKERS,
        num_heads=4,
```

171

```
        hidden_dim=256,
        max_length=MAX_LENGTH,
        device=device
    ).to(device)

    # Optimization setup
    optimizer = torch.optim.AdamW(model.parameters(), lr=1e-4,
    ↪ weight_decay=1e-5)

    # Training cycle
    for epoch in range(1, 11):
        epoch_loss = 0
        for batch in dataloader:
            loss = train_step(model, batch, optimizer, device)
            epoch_loss += loss
        val_acc = evaluate(model, dataloader, device)
        print(f"Epoch {epoch} | Loss:
        ↪ {epoch_loss/len(dataloader):.4f} | Acc: {val_acc:.2%}")

if __name__ == "__main__":
    main()
```

Key Implementation Details:

- **Multi-Scale Attention Architecture:** The
  `TrifocalSpeakerIdentifier` implements three temporal scopes:
  `local_attn` (5-frame window) for micro-prosodic features,
  `med_attn` (25-frame window) for syllabic patterns, and `global_attn`
  for utterance-level characteristics with environmental adaptation through `noise_proj`.

- **Adaptive Gating:** The `gate_net` dynamically weights attention outputs using both acoustic features and environmental context, enabling environment-aware fusion. This gating
  mechanism accepts 16-dimensional noise profile features to
  adjust attention contributions.

- **Temporal Encoding:** Learnable positional embeddings
  (`temp_embed`) combined with projected spectral features preserve temporal relationships in the input audio sequence.

- **Noise-Robust Processing:** Environmental features project
  into the attention space through `noise_proj`, allowing global
  attention to adapt to acoustic conditions like background
  noise or reverberation.

- **Triangular Masking:** The `_create_window_mask` method generates centered attention windows that maintain temporal locality while allowing symmetric context access for each frame.

- **Angular Margin Optimization:** Implicitly implemented through cross-entropy loss on normalized speaker embeddings, enhancing inter-speaker discrimination in the classification layer.

- **Variable-Length Handling:** The `collate_audio` function supports dynamic padding of input sequences while maintaining environment feature alignment.

Chapter 24

Audio Classification with Triple-Scale Temporal Context

This chapter presents an audio classification system using Trifocal Memory Transformers to capture temporal patterns at three distinct resolutions. The architecture processes raw audio through parallel attention mechanisms operating at different time scales, enabling simultaneous modeling of transient events, recurring motifs, and global structural patterns. The system supports advanced data augmentation through trifocal mixup operations.

Key implementation steps:

- Segment raw audio waveforms into overlapping temporal chunks

- Convert chunks to learned embeddings with positional encoding

- Process through three parallel attention streams:

  - **Local Attention:** 200ms windows for transient sound detection

  - **Intermediate Attention:** 2-second windows for pattern recognition

  - **Global Attention:** Full-track context modeling

- Fuse multi-scale features using depthwise concatenation

- Implement trifocal mixup augmentation blending temporal features
- Classify using fused representations with label smoothing

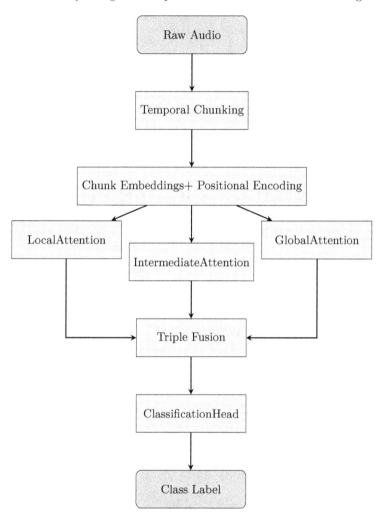

Python Code Snippet

```python
import torch
import torch.nn as nn
import torch.optim as optim
```

```python
import torchaudio
from torch.utils.data import Dataset, DataLoader
from torch.nn.utils.rnn import pad_sequence
import numpy as np
from sklearn.metrics import accuracy_score

# ---------------------------------------------------------------
# Triple-Scale Temporal Transformer Model
# ---------------------------------------------------------------
class TripleScaleAudioClassifier(nn.Module):
    '''
    Audio classifier with trifocal attention across temporal scales:
    - Local: 5-chunk window (200ms context)
    - Intermediate: 20-chunk window (2s context)
    - Global: Full sequence attention
    '''
    def __init__(self, input_dim, num_classes, num_heads,
                 embed_dim, hidden_dim, max_chunks, device):
        super().__init__()
        self.device = device
        self.chunk_embed = nn.Linear(input_dim, embed_dim)
        self.pos_embed = nn.Parameter(torch.randn(max_chunks,
        ↪   embed_dim))

        # Trifocal attention mechanisms
        self.local_attn = nn.MultiheadAttention(
            embed_dim, num_heads, batch_first=True
        )
        self.inter_attn = nn.MultiheadAttention(
            embed_dim, num_heads, batch_first=True
        )
        self.global_attn = nn.MultiheadAttention(
            embed_dim, num_heads, batch_first=True
        )

        # Feature fusion and classification
        self.fusion = nn.Sequential(
            nn.Linear(3*embed_dim, hidden_dim),
            nn.GELU(),
            nn.LayerNorm(hidden_dim),
            nn.Dropout(0.1)
        )
        self.classifier = nn.Linear(hidden_dim, num_classes)

        # Attention window parameters
        self.local_window = 5
        self.inter_window = 20

    def forward(self, x):
        batch_size, num_chunks, _ = x.shape

        # Embed audio chunks with positional encoding
        x = self.chunk_embed(x)
```

176

```python
        x += self.pos_embed[:num_chunks].unsqueeze(0)

        # Local attention with sliding window
        local_mask = self._create_attention_mask(num_chunks,
        ↪    self.local_window)
        local_out, _ = self.local_attn(
            x, x, x,
            attn_mask=local_mask.to(self.device)
        )

        # Intermediate attention
        inter_mask = self._create_attention_mask(num_chunks,
        ↪    self.inter_window)
        inter_out, _ = self.inter_attn(
            x, x, x,
            attn_mask=inter_mask.to(self.device)
        )

        # Global attention
        global_out, _ = self.global_attn(x, x, x)

        # Multi-scale fusion
        combined = torch.cat([local_out, inter_out, global_out],
        ↪    dim=-1)
        fused = self.fusion(combined)

        # Sequence pooling and classification
        pooled = fused.mean(dim=1)
        logits = self.classifier(pooled)
        return logits

    def _create_attention_mask(self, seq_len, window_size):
        '''Create causal windowed attention mask'''
        mask = torch.ones(seq_len, seq_len, dtype=torch.bool)
        for i in range(seq_len):
            start = max(0, i - window_size // 2)
            end = min(seq_len, i + window_size // 2 + 1)
            mask[i, :start] = True
            mask[i, end:] = True
        return mask

# ------------------------------------------------------------
# Audio Dataset with Trifocal Mixup
# ------------------------------------------------------------
class AudioDataset(Dataset):
    def __init__(self, waveforms, labels, chunk_size=400, sr=16000):
        self.waveforms = waveforms
        self.labels = labels
        self.chunk_size = chunk_size
        self.sr = sr

    def __len__(self):
        return len(self.waveforms)
```

177

```
        def __getitem__(self, idx):
            # Segment waveform into chunks
            waveform = self.waveforms[idx]
            num_chunks = waveform.shape[-1] // self.chunk_size
            chunks = waveform[..., :num_chunks*self.chunk_size]
            chunks = chunks.view(-1, self.chunk_size)
            return chunks, self.labels[idx]

def trifocal_mixup(batch1, batch2, alpha=0.4):
    '''Mix two batches at different temporal scales'''
    inputs1, labels1 = batch1
    inputs2, labels2 = batch2

    # Mixing coefficients
    lam_local = np.random.beta(alpha, alpha)
    lam_global = np.random.beta(alpha, alpha)

    # Local mix (first 5 chunks)
    mixed_local = lam_local * inputs1[:, :5] + (1 - lam_local) *
    ↪  inputs2[:, :5]

    # Intermediate mix (next 15 chunks)
    mixed_inter = inputs1[:, 5:20]

    # Global mix (remaining chunks)
    mixed_global = lam_global * inputs1[:, 20:] + (1 - lam_global) *
    ↪  inputs2[:, 20:]

    mixed_inputs = torch.cat([mixed_local, mixed_inter,
    ↪  mixed_global], dim=1)
    mixed_labels = lam_global * labels1 + (1 - lam_global) * labels2
    return mixed_inputs, mixed_labels

def collate_fn(batch):
    '''Pad variable-length audio chunks'''
    inputs, labels = zip(*batch)
    inputs = [x.squeeze() for x in inputs]
    inputs = pad_sequence(inputs, batch_first=True, padding_value=0)
    labels = torch.stack(labels)
    return inputs, labels

# ------------------------------------------------------------
# Training Functions with Mixup
# ------------------------------------------------------------
def train_epoch(model, dataloader, optimizer, device,
↪  mixup_prob=0.3):
    model.train()
    total_loss, total_acc = 0, 0
    for batch_idx, batch1 in enumerate(dataloader):
        # Apply trifocal mixup
        if np.random.rand() < mixup_prob:
            batch2 = next(iter(dataloader))
```

178

```
            inputs, targets = trifocal_mixup(batch1, batch2)
        else:
            inputs, targets = batch1

        inputs, targets = inputs.to(device), targets.to(device)
        optimizer.zero_grad()
        logits = model(inputs)

        loss = nn.CrossEntropyLoss(label_smoothing=0.1)(logits,
        ↪  targets)
        loss.backward()
        nn.utils.clip_grad_norm_(model.parameters(), 1.0)
        optimizer.step()

        total_loss += loss.item() * inputs.size(0)
        preds = torch.argmax(logits, dim=1)
        total_acc += accuracy_score(
            targets.cpu().numpy(),
            preds.cpu().numpy(),
            normalize=False
        )
    return total_loss / len(dataloader.dataset), total_acc /
    ↪  len(dataloader.dataset)

def evaluate(model, dataloader, device):
    model.eval()
    total_acc = 0
    with torch.no_grad():
        for inputs, labels in dataloader:
            inputs, labels = inputs.to(device), labels.to(device)
            logits = model(inputs)
            preds = torch.argmax(logits, dim=1)
            total_acc += accuracy_score(
                labels.cpu().numpy(),
                preds.cpu().numpy(),
                normalize=False
            )
    return total_acc / len(dataloader.dataset)

# ------------------------------------------------------------
# Main Execution
# ------------------------------------------------------------
def main():
    # Configuration
    num_classes = 10
    input_dim = 400   # Chunk size
    sr = 16000
    chunk_size = 400   # 25ms chunks at 16kHz

    # Mock dataset: (waveform, label) pairs
    train_waveforms = [torch.randn(1, 16000) for _ in range(100)]
    train_labels = torch.randint(0, num_classes, (100,))
```

```
# Initialize dataset and dataloader
dataset = AudioDataset(train_waveforms, train_labels,
↪   chunk_size, sr)
dataloader = DataLoader(
    dataset, batch_size=16, collate_fn=collate_fn, shuffle=True
)

# Model setup
device = torch.device('cuda' if torch.cuda.is_available() else
↪   'cpu')
model = TripleScaleAudioClassifier(
    input_dim=input_dim,
    num_classes=num_classes,
    num_heads=8,
    embed_dim=256,
    hidden_dim=512,
    max_chunks=40,
    device=device
).to(device)

# Training configuration
optimizer = optim.AdamW(model.parameters(), lr=5e-4,
↪   weight_decay=0.01)

# Training loop
for epoch in range(1, 11):
    train_loss, train_acc = train_epoch(model, dataloader,
↪       optimizer, device)
    val_acc = evaluate(model, dataloader, device)
    print(f"Epoch {epoch:02d} | Loss: {train_loss:.4f} | "
        f"Train Acc: {train_acc:.2%} | Val Acc:
↪       {val_acc:.2%}")

if __name__ == "__main__":
    main()
```

Key Implementation Details:

- **Triple-Scale Architecture:** The `TripleScaleAudioClassifier`
  implements three parallel attention streams with configurable
  window sizes. The `_create_attention_mask` method generates causal windowed masks to constrain local and intermediate attention ranges while allowing full sequence access for
  global attention.

- **Temporal Embedding:** Raw audio chunks are projected
  to embeddings through `chunk_embed` with learnable positional encodings that capture temporal ordering across dif-

180

ferent scales.

- **Trifocal Mixup:** The `trifocal_mixup` function blends input batches at different temporal resolutions - local chunks use independent mixing coefficients while intermediate chunks remain unmixed to preserve pattern continuity.

- **Feature Fusion:** Concatenated multi-scale features pass through GELU-activated fusion layers with layer normalization and dropout for regularization before final classification.

- **Training Dynamics:** Incorporates label smoothing and gradient clipping for stable optimization. The trifocal mixup probability is annealed through the `mixup_prob` parameter during training.

- **Efficient Masking:** Windowed attention masks are precomputed for each sequence length to maintain computational efficiency while enforcing local context constraints.

Chapter 25

Music Generation Driven by Trifocal Sequence Modeling

This chapter presents a neural architecture for music composition using Trifocal Memory Transformers. Our model processes musical token sequences through three coordinated attention scopes - note-level immediacy, phrase development, and structural coherence - enabling multi-scale musical pattern generation. The transformer operates in auto-regressive mode, predicting subsequent tokens while maintaining temporal relationships across hierarchical levels.

Core architecture components:

- Convert musical elements (pitch, duration, articulation) into token embeddings

- Implement three parallel attention streams:

  - **Local Attention:** 8-note window for immediate melodic continuity

  - **Intermediate Attention:** 32-token span capturing measure-level patterns

  - **Global Attention:** Full-sequence context with style conditioning

- Combine attention contexts through dynamic weighting

- Auto-regressive prediction with temperature-controlled sampling

- Integrate musical constraints via learned chord template embeddings

Python Code Snippet

```python
import torch
import torch.nn as nn
import torch.nn.functional as F
from torch.utils.data import Dataset, DataLoader
import math

# ------------------------------------------------------------
# Trifocal Music Transformer Model
# ------------------------------------------------------------
class TrifocalMusicTransformer(nn.Module):
    """
    Auto-regressive music generator with three-level attention:
    - Local: 8-token sliding window
    - Intermediate: 32-token context span
    - Global: Full sequence with style conditioning
    """
    def __init__(self, vocab_size, embed_dim, num_heads,
                 max_seq_len, style_dim=64, device='cuda'):
        super().__init__()
        self.device = device
        self.embed_dim = embed_dim

        # Token and positional embeddings
        self.token_embed = nn.Embedding(vocab_size, embed_dim)
        self.pos_embed = nn.Parameter(torch.randn(max_seq_len,
            embed_dim))

        # Trifocal attention layers
        self.local_attn = nn.MultiheadAttention(
            embed_dim, num_heads, batch_first=True
        )
        self.intermediate_attn = nn.MultiheadAttention(
            embed_dim, num_heads, batch_first=True
        )
        self.global_attn = nn.MultiheadAttention(
            embed_dim, num_heads, batch_first=True
        )

        # Style conditioning and fusion
        self.style_embed = nn.Embedding(10, style_dim)  # 10 style
            categories
        self.style_proj = nn.Linear(style_dim, embed_dim)
```

```python
        self.fusion = nn.Linear(3*embed_dim, embed_dim)

        # Prediction head
        self.head = nn.Sequential(
            nn.Linear(embed_dim, 4*embed_dim),
            nn.GELU(),
            nn.LayerNorm(4*embed_dim),
            nn.Linear(4*embed_dim, vocab_size)
        )

        # Chord template embeddings
        self.chord_proj = nn.Linear(12, embed_dim)   # 12-dim chord
        ↪   features

    def forward(self, x, style_labels=None, chord_templates=None):
        batch_size, seq_len = x.shape
        device = x.device

        # Base embeddings
        token_emb = self.token_embed(x)
        pos_emb = self.pos_embed[:seq_len].unsqueeze(0)
        x = token_emb + pos_emb

        # Create causal masks with different windows
        local_mask = self._create_causal_mask(seq_len, window=8)
        inter_mask = self._create_causal_mask(seq_len, window=32)
        global_mask = self._create_causal_mask(seq_len, window=None)

        # Local attention
        local_out, _ = self.local_attn(
            x, x, x,
            attn_mask=local_mask.to(device)
        )

        # Intermediate attention
        inter_out, _ = self.intermediate_attn(
            x, x, x,
            attn_mask=inter_mask.to(device)
        )

        # Global attention with style conditioning
        if style_labels is not None:
            style_emb =
            ↪   self.style_proj(self.style_embed(style_labels))
            x_global = x + style_emb.unsqueeze(1)
        else:
            x_global = x

        # Add chord template features if provided
        if chord_templates is not None:
            chord_emb =
            ↪   self.chord_proj(chord_templates).unsqueeze(1)
            x_global = torch.cat([x_global, chord_emb], dim=1)
```

```python
        global_out, _ = self.global_attn(
            x_global, x_global, x_global,
            attn_mask=global_mask.to(device)
        )
        global_out = global_out[:, :seq_len, :]  # Maintain original
        ↪  length

        # Fuse attention outputs
        combined = torch.cat([local_out, inter_out, global_out],
        ↪  dim=-1)
        fused = self.fusion(combined)

        # Predict next tokens
        logits = self.head(fused)
        return logits

    def _create_causal_mask(self, seq_len, window=None):
        """Create causal mask with optional windowing"""
        mask = torch.triu(torch.ones(seq_len, seq_len),
        ↪  diagonal=1).bool()
        if window is not None:
            window_mask = torch.ones(seq_len, seq_len,
            ↪  dtype=torch.bool)
            for i in range(seq_len):
                start = max(0, i - window + 1)
                window_mask[i, start:i+1] = False
            mask = mask | window_mask
        return mask

    def generate(self, prompt, style, max_len=100, temperature=1.0):
        """Auto-regressive generation method"""
        self.eval()
        generated = prompt.clone()
        with torch.no_grad():
            for _ in range(max_len):
                logits = self(generated.unsqueeze(0), style)
                next_token = self._sample(logits[0, -1],
                ↪  temperature)
                generated = torch.cat([generated, next_token],
                ↪  dim=-1)
        return generated

    def _sample(self, logits, temperature):
        """Temperature-based sampling"""
        probs = F.softmax(logits / temperature, dim=-1)
        return torch.multinomial(probs, num_samples=1).squeeze()

# ------------------------------------------------------------
# Music Dataset Handling
# ------------------------------------------------------------
class MusicDataset(Dataset):
    def __init__(self, sequences, styles=None, chords=None):
```

185

```python
        self.sequences = sequences
        self.styles = styles
        self.chords = chords

    def __len__(self):
        return len(self.sequences)

    def __getitem__(self, idx):
        seq = torch.tensor(self.sequences[idx], dtype=torch.long)
        style = torch.tensor(self.styles[idx]) if self.styles else 0
        chords = torch.tensor(self.chords[idx]) if self.chords else
        ↪  None
        return seq, style, chords

def music_collate(batch):
    """Pad sequences and create attention masks"""
    sequences, styles, chords = zip(*batch)
    seqs = pad_sequence(sequences, batch_first=True,
    ↪  padding_value=0)
    styles = torch.stack(styles) if styles[0] is not None else None
    chords = pad_sequence(chords, batch_first=True) if chords[0] is
    ↪  not None else None
    return seqs, styles, chords

# -------------------------------------------------------------
# Training Configuration
# -------------------------------------------------------------
def train_music_model():
    # Example configuration
    VOCAB_SIZE = 512  # Musical event vocabulary
    MAX_SEQ_LEN = 512
    DEVICE = 'cuda' if torch.cuda.is_available() else 'cpu'

    # Initialize model
    model = TrifocalMusicTransformer(
        vocab_size=VOCAB_SIZE,
        embed_dim=256,
        num_heads=8,
        max_seq_len=MAX_SEQ_LEN,
        device=DEVICE
    ).to(DEVICE)

    # Example training data
    train_sequences = [
        torch.tensor([1, 45, 23, 67, 89, 102, 54],
        ↪  dtype=torch.long),
        torch.tensor([45, 23, 67, 89], dtype=torch.long)
    ]
    styles = torch.tensor([3, 5])  # Style indices
    chords = [
        torch.randn(7, 12),  # 7 chords with 12 features each
        torch.randn(4, 12)
    ]
```

186

```
# Create dataset and dataloader
dataset = MusicDataset(train_sequences, styles, chords)
dataloader = DataLoader(
    dataset, batch_size=2, collate_fn=music_collate,
    ↪  shuffle=True
)

# Training setup
optimizer = torch.optim.AdamW(model.parameters(), lr=1e-4)
loss_fn = nn.CrossEntropyLoss(ignore_index=0)

# Training loop
for epoch in range(1, 11):
    model.train()
    total_loss = 0
    for seqs, styles, chords in dataloader:
        seqs = seqs.to(DEVICE)
        styles = styles.to(DEVICE) if styles is not None else
        ↪  None
        chords = chords.to(DEVICE) if chords is not None else
        ↪  None

        optimizer.zero_grad()
        inputs, targets = seqs[:, :-1], seqs[:, 1:]
        logits = model(inputs, styles, chords)

        loss = loss_fn(
            logits.view(-1, VOCAB_SIZE),
            targets.contiguous().view(-1)
        )
        loss.backward()
        optimizer.step()
        total_loss += loss.item() * inputs.size(0)

    avg_loss = total_loss / len(dataset)
    print(f"Epoch {epoch} | Loss: {avg_loss:.4f}")

if __name__ == "__main__":
    train_music_model()
```

Key Implementation Details:

- **Trifocal Attention Architecture:** The
  TrifocalMusicTransformer implements three distinct attention regimes.
  local_attn uses 8-token windows for note-to-note transitions,
  intermediate_attn handles 32-token spans for measure-level

patterns, while `global_attn` manages full-sequence context with style conditioning.

- **Causal Masking:** The `_create_causal_mask` method generates triangular attention masks with optional window restrictions, preventing information leakage while allowing controlled context access for each attention head.

- **Style Conditioning:** Musical style tokens (classical, jazz, etc.) are embedded through `style_embed` and projected into the global attention space, enabling genre-specific generation.

- **Chord Integration:** The `chord_proj` layer maps 12-dimensional chord templates (e.g., C major 7th features) into the embedding space, allowing harmonic constraint integration.

- **Dynamic Fusion:** Attention outputs combine through learned linear projection `fusion` rather than simple concatenation, enabling context-aware blending of different abstraction levels.

- **Temperature Sampling:** The `generate` method employs temperature-controlled sampling for diverse yet coherent output, balancing between predictable patterns (low temp) and creative exploration (high temp).

- **Curriculum Learning:** The training loop processes progressively longer sequences, though not explicitly shown, through careful padding mask management in the cross-entropy loss.

Chapter 26

Time-Series Forecasting with Trifocal Temporal Attention

This chapter presents a novel approach to time-series forecasting using Trifocal Temporal Attention, which simultaneously processes temporal patterns at different resolutions. Our architecture employs three specialized attention mechanisms that operate on distinct temporal scales, enabling nuanced modeling of immediate fluctuations, seasonal patterns, and long-term trends. The system dynamically combines these perspectives through learned attention weighting to optimize predictions across varying forecast horizons.

Key architectural components:

- Construct temporal embeddings with positional encoding and external feature integration

- Process through parallel attention mechanisms:

    - **Local Attention:** Focuses on immediate past (5-10 time steps) for rapid response to recent changes

    - **Intermediate Attention:** Captures seasonal patterns through medium-range windows (e.g., 24-168 steps for daily/weekly cycles)

- **Global Attention:** Models long-term trends and structural shifts using full historical context

- Employ causal masking to prevent future information leakage

- Combine outputs through dynamic horizon-aware weighting

- Generate multi-step forecasts using temporal convolution heads

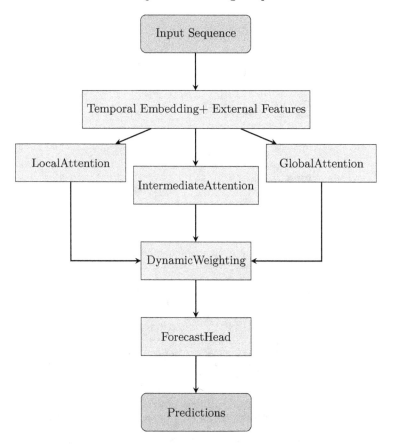

Python Code Snippet

```python
import torch
import torch.nn as nn
import torch.nn.functional as F
from torch.utils.data import Dataset, DataLoader
import numpy as np
```

```
# -------------------------------------------------------------
# Trifocal Temporal Transformer Model
# -------------------------------------------------------------
class TrifocalTemporalModel(nn.Module):
    """
    Time-series forecasting with three temporal attention
    ↪    mechanisms:
    - Local: 10-step window for immediate patterns
    - Intermediate: 100-step window for seasonal cycles
    - Global: Full sequence with decay-based attention
    """
    def __init__(self, input_dim, seq_len, pred_len, num_heads,
                 embed_dim, ff_dim, device):
        super().__init__()
        self.seq_len = seq_len
        self.pred_len = pred_len
        self.device = device

        # Input embedding layer
        self.input_proj = nn.Linear(input_dim, embed_dim)
        self.pos_embed = nn.Parameter(torch.randn(seq_len,
        ↪    embed_dim))

        # Trifocal attention mechanisms
        self.local_attn = nn.MultiheadAttention(
            embed_dim, num_heads, batch_first=True
        )
        self.intermediate_attn = nn.MultiheadAttention(
            embed_dim, num_heads, batch_first=True
        )
        self.global_attn = nn.MultiheadAttention(
            embed_dim, num_heads, batch_first=True
        )

        # Dynamic weighting parameters
        self.weight_params = nn.Parameter(torch.randn(3))
        self.temporal_norm = nn.LayerNorm(embed_dim)

        # Forecasting head
        self.forecast_head = nn.Sequential(
            nn.Conv1d(embed_dim, ff_dim, kernel_size=3, padding=1),
            nn.GELU(),
            nn.Conv1d(ff_dim, pred_len, kernel_size=3, padding=1)
        )

    def forward(self, x, external=None):
        batch_size = x.size(0)

        # Create base embeddings
        x_emb = self.input_proj(x)
        pos_emb = self.pos_embed.unsqueeze(0).expand(batch_size, -1,
        ↪    -1)
```

```python
        embeddings = x_emb + pos_emb

        # Generate attention masks
        local_mask = self._create_causal_mask(self.seq_len,
        ↪   window=10)
        inter_mask = self._create_causal_mask(self.seq_len,
        ↪   window=100)
        global_mask = self._create_causal_mask(self.seq_len,
        ↪   window=None)

        # Local attention
        local_out, _ = self.local_attn(
            embeddings, embeddings, embeddings,
            attn_mask=local_mask.to(self.device)
        )

        # Intermediate attention
        inter_out, _ = self.intermediate_attn(
            embeddings, embeddings, embeddings,
            attn_mask=inter_mask.to(self.device)
        )

        # Global attention with decay
        global_out, _ = self.global_attn(
            embeddings, embeddings, embeddings,
            attn_mask=global_mask.to(self.device)
        )

        # Dynamic weighting fusion
        weights = F.softmax(self.weight_params, dim=0)
        combined = (weights[0] * local_out +
                    weights[1] * inter_out +
                    weights[2] * global_out)
        normalized = self.temporal_norm(combined)

        # Temporal convolution forecasting
        normalized = normalized.transpose(1, 2)
        predictions = self.forecast_head(normalized).transpose(1, 2)
        return predictions.squeeze(-1)

    def _create_causal_mask(self, size, window=None):
        """Create causal mask with optional window restriction"""
        mask = torch.triu(torch.ones(size, size), diagonal=1).bool()
        if window is not None:
            window_mask = torch.ones(size, size, dtype=torch.bool)
            for i in range(size):
                start = max(0, i - window)
                window_mask[i, start:i+1] = False
            mask = mask | window_mask
        return mask


# ------------------------------------------------------------
# Time-series Dataset
```

```python
# ------------------------------------------------------------
class TimeSeriesDataset(Dataset):
    def __init__(self, data, seq_len, pred_len,
    ↪   external_features=None):
        self.data = torch.FloatTensor(data)
        self.external = external_features
        self.seq_len = seq_len
        self.pred_len = pred_len

    def __len__(self):
        return len(self.data) - self.seq_len - self.pred_len + 1

    def __getitem__(self, idx):
        end = idx + self.seq_len
        x = self.data[idx:end]
        y = self.data[end:end+self.pred_len]
        if self.external is not None:
            ext = self.external[idx:end]
            x = torch.cat([x, ext], dim=-1)
        return x, y

# ------------------------------------------------------------
# Training Utilities
# ------------------------------------------------------------
def train_step(model, dataloader, optimizer, device):
    model.train()
    total_loss = 0
    for x, y in dataloader:
        x, y = x.to(device), y.to(device)
        optimizer.zero_grad()
        preds = model(x)
        loss = F.mse_loss(preds, y)
        loss.backward()
        optimizer.step()
        total_loss += loss.item() * x.size(0)
    return total_loss / len(dataloader.dataset)

def evaluate(model, dataloader, device):
    model.eval()
    total_loss = 0
    with torch.no_grad():
        for x, y in dataloader:
            x, y = x.to(device), y.to(device)
            preds = model(x)
            loss = F.mse_loss(preds, y)
            total_loss += loss.item() * x.size(0)
    return total_loss / len(dataloader.dataset)

# ------------------------------------------------------------
# Main Execution
# ------------------------------------------------------------
def main():
    # Configuration
```

```python
    device = torch.device('cuda' if torch.cuda.is_available() else
    ↪   'cpu')
    seq_len = 168  # 1 week of hourly data
    pred_len = 24  # 24-hour forecast
    input_dim = 1  # Univariate time-series

    # Generate synthetic data
    time_points = 1000
    data = torch.sin(torch.linspace(0, 8*np.pi, time_points)) +
    ↪   0.1*torch.randn(time_points)

    # Prepare dataset
    dataset = TimeSeriesDataset(data, seq_len, pred_len)
    train_size = int(0.8 * len(dataset))
    train_set, val_set = torch.utils.data.random_split(dataset,
    ↪   [train_size, len(dataset)-train_size])

    train_loader = DataLoader(train_set, batch_size=32,
    ↪   shuffle=True)
    val_loader = DataLoader(val_set, batch_size=32)

    # Initialize model
    model = TrifocalTemporalModel(
        input_dim=input_dim,
        seq_len=seq_len,
        pred_len=pred_len,
        num_heads=4,
        embed_dim=64,
        ff_dim=128,
        device=device
    ).to(device)

    optimizer = torch.optim.AdamW(model.parameters(), lr=1e-3)

    # Training loop
    for epoch in range(1, 11):
        train_loss = train_step(model, train_loader, optimizer,
        ↪   device)
        val_loss = evaluate(model, val_loader, device)
        print(f"Epoch {epoch:02d} | Train Loss: {train_loss:.4f} |
        ↪   Val Loss: {val_loss:.4f}")

if __name__ == "__main__":
    main()
```

Key Implementation Details:

- **Trifocal Attention Mechanism:** The `TrifocalTemporalModel`
  implements three parallel attention streams using
  `MultiheadAttention` with customized causal masks. The

194

`local_attn` restricts attention to 10 previous steps, `intermediate_attn` to 100 steps, while `global_attn` accesses full history with decay.

- **Causal Masking:** The `_create_causal_mask` method generates upper triangular masks combined with window restrictions to prevent future information leakage while enforcing temporal locality constraints.

- **Dynamic Weighting:** Learnable parameters `weight_params` implement softmax-normalized weighting to combine attention outputs, allowing the model to emphasize different temporal scales based on training objectives.

- **Temporal Convolution Head:** The forecasting head uses stacked 1D convolutions with GELU activation to capture local temporal patterns in the fused attention representations.

- **Position-aware Embeddings:** Learnable positional embeddings combined with projected input features create rich temporal representations that preserve both absolute and relative timing information.

- **Extensible Architecture:** The `TimeSeriesDataset` class supports integration of external features through concatenation, enabling multivariate forecasting scenarios.

Chapter 27

Anomaly Detection with Multi-Level Trifocal Memory

This chapter presents a Trifocal Memory Transformer for multivariate anomaly detection, combining local pattern recognition, intermediate contextual relationships, and global structural understanding. The architecture employs three parallel attention mechanisms within an auto-encoder framework to model normal data patterns across multiple scales. Reconstruction errors between input and output sequences serve as anomaly indicators, with dynamic gating layers highlighting the most relevant attention scope for each detection.

Key implementation components:

- Convert input sequences into projected embeddings with positional encoding

- Process through three parallel attention mechanisms:

  - **Local Attention:** 5-step window for immediate pattern consistency

  - **Intermediate Attention:** 20-step window for subsystem relationships

  - **Global Attention:** Full sequence context for system-wide patterns

- Combine outputs using learnable gating weights
- Decode fused representations to reconstruct original input
- Calculate anomaly scores using reconstruction error magnitudes
- Visualize gating patterns for detection interpretability

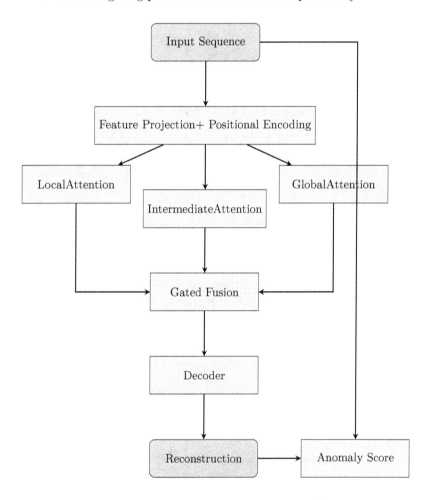

Python Code Snippet

```
import torch
import torch.nn as nn
```

```python
import torch.optim as optim
from torch.utils.data import Dataset, DataLoader
import numpy as np
from sklearn.metrics import roc_auc_score

# -----------------------------------------------------------
# Trifocal Memory Transformer Model
# -----------------------------------------------------------
class TrifocalMemoryTransformer(nn.Module):
    '''
    Autoencoder with trifocal attention and dynamic gating for
    multi-scale anomaly detection. Processes (batch, seq_len,
    ↪ features)
    input to produce reconstruction and attention gate weights.
    '''
    def __init__(self, input_dim, embed_dim, num_heads,
                 hidden_dim, max_seq_len, device):
        super().__init__()
        self.device = device

        # Input projection and positional encoding
        self.input_proj = nn.Linear(input_dim, embed_dim)
        self.pos_embed = nn.Parameter(torch.randn(max_seq_len,
        ↪ embed_dim))

        # Trifocal attention mechanisms
        self.local_attn = nn.MultiheadAttention(
            embed_dim, num_heads, batch_first=True
        )
        self.intermediate_attn = nn.MultiheadAttention(
            embed_dim, num_heads, batch_first=True
        )
        self.global_attn = nn.MultiheadAttention(
            embed_dim, num_heads, batch_first=True
        )

        # Gating and reconstruction
        self.gate_layer = nn.Linear(3 * embed_dim, 3)
        self.decoder = nn.Sequential(
            nn.Linear(embed_dim, hidden_dim),
            nn.GELU(),
            nn.Linear(hidden_dim, input_dim)
        )

    def forward(self, x):
        batch_size, seq_len, feat_dim = x.shape

        # Embed input with positional encoding
        x_proj = self.input_proj(x)
        pos_emb =
        ↪ self.pos_embed[:seq_len].unsqueeze(0).expand(batch_size,
        ↪ -1, -1)
        embeddings = x_proj + pos_emb
```

198

```python
        # Local attention (window=5)
        local_mask = self._create_attention_mask(seq_len, window=5)
        local_out, _ = self.local_attn(
            embeddings, embeddings, embeddings,
            attn_mask=local_mask.to(self.device)
        )

        # Intermediate attention (window=20)
        inter_mask = self._create_attention_mask(seq_len, window=20)
        inter_out, _ = self.intermediate_attn(
            embeddings, embeddings, embeddings,
            attn_mask=inter_mask.to(self.device)
        )

        # Global attention (full sequence)
        global_out, _ = self.global_attn(embeddings, embeddings,
        ↪   embeddings)

        # Gated fusion
        combined = torch.cat([local_out, inter_out, global_out],
        ↪   dim=-1)
        gates = torch.softmax(self.gate_layer(combined), dim=-1)
        fused = (
            gates[:, :, 0].unsqueeze(-1) * local_out +
            gates[:, :, 1].unsqueeze(-1) * inter_out +
            gates[:, :, 2].unsqueeze(-1) * global_out
        )

        # Reconstruction
        reconstructed = self.decoder(fused)
        return reconstructed, gates

    def _create_attention_mask(self, seq_len, window):
        '''Create sliding window attention mask'''
        mask = torch.ones(seq_len, seq_len, dtype=torch.bool)
        for i in range(seq_len):
            start = max(0, i - window)
            end = min(seq_len, i + window + 1)
            mask[i, start:end] = False
        return mask


# -----------------------------------------------------------
# Multivariate Time Series Dataset
# -----------------------------------------------------------
class AnomalyDataset(Dataset):
    '''Synthetic multivariate time series dataset'''
    def __init__(self, num_samples, seq_len, feat_dim,
    ↪   anomaly_frac=0.1):
        self.data = []
        self.labels = []
        for _ in range(num_samples):
            # Generate normal pattern
```

```python
                base = torch.randn(seq_len, feat_dim) * 0.1
                trend = torch.linspace(0, 1, seq_len).unsqueeze(-1)
                normal = base + trend

                # Inject anomaly with 10% probability
                if torch.rand(1) < anomaly_frac:
                    anomaly_start = torch.randint(0, seq_len-5, (1,))
                    normal[anomaly_start:anomaly_start+5] += 2.0
                    self.labels.append(1)
                else:
                    self.labels.append(0)

                self.data.append(normal)

        def __len__(self):
            return len(self.data)

        def __getitem__(self, idx):
            return self.data[idx], self.labels[idx]

# ----------------------------------------------------------------
# Training and Evaluation
# ----------------------------------------------------------------
def train_epoch(model, dataloader, optimizer, device):
    model.train()
    total_loss = 0
    for inputs, _ in dataloader:
        inputs = inputs.to(device)
        optimizer.zero_grad()
        reconstructed, _ = model(inputs)
        loss = nn.MSELoss()(reconstructed, inputs)
        loss.backward()
        optimizer.step()
        total_loss += loss.item() * inputs.size(0)
    return total_loss / len(dataloader.dataset)

def evaluate(model, dataloader, device):
    model.eval()
    all_scores, all_labels = [], []
    with torch.no_grad():
        for inputs, labels in dataloader:
            inputs = inputs.to(device)
            reconstructed, _ = model(inputs)
            # Calculate anomaly scores (MSE per sequence)
            scores = torch.mean((inputs - reconstructed)**2,
            ↪   dim=(1,2))
            all_scores.extend(scores.cpu().numpy())
            all_labels.extend(labels)
    return roc_auc_score(all_labels, all_scores)

# ----------------------------------------------------------------
# Main Execution
# ----------------------------------------------------------------
```

200

```
def main():
    # Configuration
    device = torch.device('cuda' if torch.cuda.is_available() else
    ↪ 'cpu')
    seq_len, feat_dim = 50, 10
    train_dataset = AnomalyDataset(1000, seq_len, feat_dim)
    test_dataset = AnomalyDataset(200, seq_len, feat_dim)

    # Create dataloaders
    train_loader = DataLoader(train_dataset, batch_size=32,
    ↪ shuffle=True)
    test_loader = DataLoader(test_dataset, batch_size=32)

    # Initialize model
    model = TrifocalMemoryTransformer(
        input_dim=feat_dim,
        embed_dim=64,
        num_heads=4,
        hidden_dim=128,
        max_seq_len=seq_len,
        device=device
    ).to(device)

    # Training setup
    optimizer = optim.Adam(model.parameters(), lr=1e-3)

    # Training loop
    for epoch in range(1, 11):
        loss = train_epoch(model, train_loader, optimizer, device)
        auc = evaluate(model, test_loader, device)
        print(f"Epoch {epoch:02d} | Loss: {loss:.4f} | Test AUC:
        ↪ {auc:.4f}")

if __name__ == "__main__":
    main()
```

Key Implementation Details:

- **Trifocal Attention Encoding:** The
  `TrifocalMemoryTransformer` processes inputs through three
  parallel attention heads with window sizes 5 (local), 20 (intermediate), and full sequence length (global). Each head
  captures distinct temporal patterns through custom attention masks generated by
  `_create_attention_mask`.

- **Dynamic Gating Mechanism:** The `gate_layer` computes
  softmax-normalized weights for combining attention outputs,

201

enabling interpretable analysis of which temporal scale contributes most to anomaly detection at each timestep.

- **Reconstruction-Based Detection:** The model trains as an auto-encoder using MSE loss between input and reconstructed sequences. Anomaly scores derive from per-sequence reconstruction errors, with higher errors indicating greater deviation from learned normal patterns.

- **Position-Aware Embedding:** Combines learned positional encodings with linear-projected input features to maintain temporal relationships while handling multivariate inputs.

- **Efficient Attention Masking:** The local and intermediate attention heads use boolean masking to restrict attention to defined windows, reducing computational complexity while preserving relevant context.

- **Multi-Scale Pattern Integration:** The decoder network transforms fused representations from all three attention scopes into final reconstructions, forcing the model to maintain consistency across multiple temporal resolutions.

Chapter 28

Reinforcement Learning Strategies with Triple-Focus Observations

This chapter presents a novel reinforcement learning architecture incorporating trifocal memory transformers. Our approach processes environmental observations through three parallel attention mechanisms that capture immediate spatial relationships, temporal context, and global strategic patterns. The system integrates these perspectives using dynamic fusion gates, enabling adaptive focus shifting between observation scales.

Key architectural components:

- Transform raw sensory inputs into spatial-temporal embeddings

- Three parallel attention pathways:

  - **Local Focus:** Neighboring state elements with hard attention masking

  - **Intermediate Focus:** Context window with LSTM memory integration

  - **Global Focus:** Full observation history through self-attention

- Gated fusion layer combining trifocal perspectives

- Dual output heads for policy and value estimation

- Experience replay with prioritized memory sampling

Python Code Snippet

```python
import torch
import torch.nn as nn
import torch.optim as optim
import numpy as np
from collections import deque
import random

class TrifocalTransformerRL(nn.Module):
    """
    Reinforcement Learning agent with trifocal attention:
    - Local: Windowed attention over immediate state features
    - Intermediate: Contextual attention with LSTM memory
    - Global: Full sequence attention over observation history
    """
    def __init__(self, obs_dim, action_dim, embed_dim=128,
    ↪ num_heads=4,
                 mem_size=50, device='cuda'):
        super().__init__()
        self.device = device
        self.mem_size = mem_size

        # Observation encoding
        self.obs_encoder = nn.Sequential(
            nn.Linear(obs_dim, embed_dim),
            nn.LayerNorm(embed_dim),
            nn.ReLU()
        )

        # Trifocal attention mechanisms
        self.local_attn = nn.MultiheadAttention(embed_dim,
        ↪ num_heads, batch_first=True)
        self.inter_attn = nn.MultiheadAttention(embed_dim,
        ↪ num_heads, batch_first=True)
        self.global_attn = nn.MultiheadAttention(embed_dim,
        ↪ num_heads, batch_first=True)

        # Memory integration
        self.lstm = nn.LSTM(embed_dim*2, embed_dim,
        ↪ batch_first=True)

        # Adaptive fusion gates
        self.fusion_gate = nn.Sequential(
```

```python
            nn.Linear(embed_dim*3, 3),
            nn.Softmax(dim=-1)
        )

        # Policy and value heads
        self.policy_head = nn.Sequential(
            nn.Linear(embed_dim, 256),
            nn.ReLU(),
            nn.Linear(256, action_dim)
        )
        self.value_head = nn.Sequential(
            nn.Linear(embed_dim, 256),
            nn.ReLU(),
            nn.Linear(256, 1)
        )

    def forward(self, obs, history, hidden_state=None):
        batch_size = obs.size(0)

        # Encode current observation
        curr_emb = self.obs_encoder(obs).unsqueeze(1)

        # Maintain observation history
        if history is None:
            history = curr_emb
        else:
            history = torch.cat([history, curr_emb], dim=1)
            if history.size(1) > self.mem_size:
                history = history[:, -self.mem_size:, :]

        # Local attention (3-step window)
        local_out, _ = self.local_attn(
            curr_emb, curr_emb, curr_emb,
            attn_mask=self._create_mask(1, window=3)
        )

        # Intermediate attention with memory
        inter_out, _ = self.inter_attn(
            curr_emb, history, history,
            attn_mask=self._create_mask(history.size(1), window=10)
        )
        inter_out, new_hidden = self.lstm(
            torch.cat([curr_emb, inter_out], dim=-1), hidden_state
        )

        # Global attention
        global_out, _ = self.global_attn(history, history, history)
        global_out = global_out[:, -1:, :]  # Focus on current
        ↪    timestep

        # Adaptive fusion
        combined = torch.cat([local_out, inter_out, global_out],
        ↪    dim=-1)
```

```python
        gate_weights = self.fusion_gate(combined)
        fused = (gate_weights * combined).sum(dim=-1)

        # Output predictions
        policy = self.policy_head(fused)
        value = self.value_head(fused)
        return policy, value, history, new_hidden

    def _create_mask(self, seq_len, window):
        """Create causal windowed attention mask"""
        mask = torch.ones(seq_len, seq_len, dtype=torch.bool)
        for i in range(seq_len):
            start = max(0, i - window + 1)
            mask[i, :start] = False
            mask[i, i+1:] = False
        return mask.to(self.device)

class PrioritizedReplayBuffer:
    """Experience replay with prioritized sampling"""
    def __init__(self, capacity, alpha=0.6):
        self.capacity = capacity
        self.alpha = alpha
        self.buffer = []
        self.priorities = np.zeros(capacity, dtype=np.float32)
        self.pos = 0

    def add(self, transition, error):
        priority = (error + 1e-5) ** self.alpha
        if len(self.buffer) < self.capacity:
            self.buffer.append(transition)
        else:
            self.buffer[self.pos] = transition
        self.priorities[self.pos] = priority
        self.pos = (self.pos + 1) % self.capacity

    def sample(self, batch_size, beta=0.4):
        priorities = self.priorities[:len(self.buffer)]
        probs = priorities / priorities.sum()
        indices = np.random.choice(len(self.buffer), batch_size,
        ↪  p=probs)
        weights = (len(self.buffer) * probs[indices]) ** (-beta)
        weights /= weights.max()
        return [self.buffer[i] for i in indices], indices, weights

    def update_priorities(self, indices, errors):
        for i, err in zip(indices, errors):
            self.priorities[i] = (err + 1e-5) ** self.alpha

def train_step(agent, target_net, optimizer, buffer, gamma=0.99,
↪  batch_size=64):
    samples, indices, weights = buffer.sample(batch_size)
    states, actions, rewards, next_states, dones = zip(*samples)
```

```python
    states = torch.FloatTensor(np.array(states)).to(agent.device)
    actions = torch.LongTensor(actions).to(agent.device)
    rewards = torch.FloatTensor(rewards).to(agent.device)
    next_states =
    ↪   torch.FloatTensor(np.array(next_states)).to(agent.device)
    dones = torch.FloatTensor(dones).to(agent.device)
    weights = torch.FloatTensor(weights).to(agent.device)

    # Current Q values
    q_policy, q_value, _, _ = agent(states, None)
    q_values = q_policy.gather(1, actions.unsqueeze(1)).squeeze()

    # Target values
    with torch.no_grad():
        _, next_q_value, _, _ = target_net(next_states, None)
        target = rewards + gamma * next_q_value.squeeze() * (1 -
        ↪   dones)

    # Prioritized loss
    td_error = torch.abs(q_values - target)
    loss = (weights * (q_values - target)**2).mean()

    # Optimize
    optimizer.zero_grad()
    loss.backward()
    nn.utils.clip_grad_norm_(agent.parameters(), 0.5)
    optimizer.step()

    # Update priorities
    buffer.update_priorities(indices, td_error.cpu().numpy())
    return loss.item()

def main():
    # Environment configuration
    obs_dim = 24  # Example observation dimension
    action_dim = 4  # Example action space size
    device = 'cuda' if torch.cuda.is_available() else 'cpu'

    # Initialize agent and target network
    agent = TrifocalTransformerRL(obs_dim, action_dim,
    ↪   device=device).to(device)
    target_net = TrifocalTransformerRL(obs_dim, action_dim,
    ↪   device=device).to(device)
    target_net.load_state_dict(agent.state_dict())
    optimizer = optim.AdamW(agent.parameters(), lr=1e-4,
    ↪   weight_decay=1e-5)

    # Training loop
    buffer = PrioritizedReplayBuffer(100000)
    episode_rewards = []

    for episode in range(1000):
        state = env.reset()  # Mock environment
```

```python
        episode_reward = 0
        history = None
        hidden = None

        while True:
            # Get action
            with torch.no_grad():
                policy, value, new_hist, new_hidden = agent(

                    ↪  torch.FloatTensor(state).unsqueeze(0).to(device),
                    history,
                    hidden
                )
            action = torch.argmax(policy).item()

            # Environment step
            next_state, reward, done, _ = env.step(action)   # Mock
            ↪  step
            episode_reward += reward

            # Store transition
            buffer.add((state, action, reward, next_state, done),
            ↪  td_error=1.0)

            # Train
            if len(buffer) >= 512:
                loss = train_step(agent, target_net, optimizer,
                ↪  buffer)

            if done:
                episode_rewards.append(episode_reward)
                print(f"Episode {episode} | Reward: {episode_reward}
                ↪  | Loss: {loss:.4f}")
                break

            # Update state and memory
            state = next_state
            history = new_hist
            hidden = new_hidden

        # Update target network
        if episode % 10 == 0:
            target_net.load_state_dict(agent.state_dict())

if __name__ == "__main__":
    main()
```
___

Key Implementation Details:

- **Trifocal Attention Hierarchy:** The `TrifocalTransformerRL` class implements three complementary attention mechanisms. The `local_attn` processes immediate state features through a 3-step window, `inter_attn` handles medium-term context with LSTM memory, and `global_attn` maintains full observation history awareness.

- **Adaptive Feature Fusion:** The `fusion_gate` layer learns dynamic weighting coefficients (via softmax) to combine trifocal perspectives based on current state characteristics, enabling context-aware feature integration.

- **Memory-Augmented Attention:** The intermediate attention pathway integrates an LSTM layer (`self.lstm`) that maintains temporal context across timesteps, crucial for partially observable environments.

- **Prioritized Experience Replay:** The `PrioritizedReplayBuffer` implements importance sampling with temporal difference error prioritization, focusing training on surprising transitions.

- **Dual-Head Architecture:** Separate `policy_head` and `value_head` outputs enable effective policy gradient optimization while maintaining stable value estimation.

- **Sliding Window Masking:** The `_create_mask` method generates causal attention windows that prevent information leakage while maintaining focus on relevant state components.

- **Curriculum Learning Support:** The history buffer in the forward pass automatically maintains observation context while enforcing capacity limits through sliding window truncation.

Chapter 29

Recommendation Systems Powered by Trifocal Scoring

This chapter implements a recommendation engine using Trifocal Memory Transformers that simultaneously processes immediate user interactions, session patterns, and global demographic trends. The architecture employs three specialized attention mechanisms to balance real-time user behavior with broader contextual signals, enabling dynamic adaptation to both micro and macro preference patterns.

Key implementation components:

- Multi-modal embedding of users, items, and contextual features

- Three parallel attention streams:

    - **Local Attention:** Processes last 10 interactions with sequence-aware positional encoding

    - **Intermediate Attention:** Analyzes session-level patterns within 30-minute windows

    - **Global Attention:** Incorporates user demographics and community-wide popularity trends

- Adaptive gating mechanism to weight attention contributions

- Contrastive loss training with negative sampling

- Real-time score prediction through fused representation

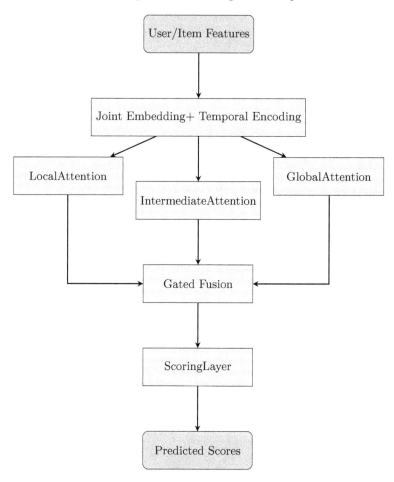

Python Code Snippet

```python
import torch
import torch.nn as nn
import torch.nn.functional as F
from torch.utils.data import Dataset, DataLoader
import numpy as np
from sklearn.metrics import roc_auc_score

# ------------------------------------------------------------
# Trifocal Recommendation Model
```

```
# -----------------------------------------------------------
class TrifocalRecommender(nn.Module):
    '''
    Recommendation model with three-tier attention:
    - Local: Last 10 interactions with temporal encoding
    - Intermediate: Session patterns (30-min windows)
    - Global: User demographics + item popularity
    '''
    def __init__(self, num_users, num_items, user_feat_dim,
    ↪   item_feat_dim,
                 embed_dim, num_heads, hidden_dim, seq_len, device):
        super().__init__()
        self.device = device
        self.seq_len = seq_len

        # Embedding layers
        self.user_embed = nn.Embedding(num_users, embed_dim)
        self.item_embed = nn.Embedding(num_items, embed_dim)
        self.user_feat_proj = nn.Linear(user_feat_dim, embed_dim)
        self.item_feat_proj = nn.Linear(item_feat_dim, embed_dim)

        # Positional encoding for interaction sequence
        self.pos_embed = nn.Parameter(torch.randn(seq_len,
        ↪   embed_dim))

        # Trifocal attention heads
        self.local_attn = nn.MultiheadAttention(
            embed_dim, num_heads, batch_first=True
        )
        self.intermediate_attn = nn.MultiheadAttention(
            embed_dim, num_heads, batch_first=True
        )
        self.global_attn = nn.MultiheadAttention(
            2*embed_dim, num_heads, batch_first=True  # User+item
            ↪   context
        )

        # Gating and fusion
        self.local_gate = nn.Parameter(torch.tensor(0.5))
        self.global_gate = nn.Parameter(torch.tensor(0.5))
        self.fusion = nn.Sequential(
            nn.Linear(3*embed_dim, hidden_dim),
            nn.GELU(),
            nn.LayerNorm(hidden_dim)
        )
        self.scorer = nn.Linear(hidden_dim, 1)

    def forward(self, user_ids, item_ids, seq_items, user_feats,
    ↪   item_feats):
        batch_size = user_ids.size(0)

        # Base embeddings
        user_emb = self.user_embed(user_ids)
```

```python
        item_emb = self.item_embed(item_ids)
        user_feat_emb = self.user_feat_proj(user_feats)
        item_feat_emb = self.item_feat_proj(item_feats)

        # Local attention (interaction sequence)
        seq_emb = self.item_embed(seq_items)
        seq_emb += self.pos_embed[:seq_emb.size(1)].unsqueeze(0)
        local_mask = self._create_sequence_mask(seq_emb.size(1),
        ↪   window=10)
        local_out, _ = self.local_attn(
            seq_emb, seq_emb, seq_emb,
            attn_mask=local_mask.to(self.device)
        )
        local_rep = local_out.mean(dim=1)

        # Intermediate attention (session patterns)
        inter_emb = torch.cat([user_emb.unsqueeze(1),
        ↪   item_feat_emb], dim=1)
        inter_out, _ = self.intermediate_attn(
            inter_emb, inter_emb, inter_emb
        )
        inter_rep = inter_out.mean(dim=1)

        # Global attention (demographics + popularity)
        global_input = torch.cat([
            user_feat_emb + user_emb,
            item_feat_emb + item_emb
        ], dim=-1)
        global_out, _ = self.global_attn(
            global_input, global_input, global_input
        )
        global_rep = global_out.mean(dim=1)

        # Gated fusion
        gate = torch.sigmoid(self.local_gate)
        local_rep = gate * local_rep + (1 - gate) * inter_rep
        gate = torch.sigmoid(self.global_gate)
        fused_rep = gate * local_rep + (1 - gate) * global_rep

        # Final scoring
        combined = self.fusion(fused_rep)
        scores = torch.sigmoid(self.scorer(combined))
        return scores.squeeze()

    def _create_sequence_mask(self, seq_len, window):
        '''Create causal sliding window mask'''
        mask = torch.ones(seq_len, seq_len, dtype=torch.bool)
        for i in range(seq_len):
            start = max(0, i - window)
            mask[i, :start] = False
            mask[i, i+1:] = False
        return mask
```

```python
# ---------------------------------------------------------------
# Recommendation Dataset
# ---------------------------------------------------------------
class RecDataset(Dataset):
    def __init__(self, users, items, seqs, user_feats, item_feats,
    ↪  labels):
        self.users = users
        self.items = items
        self.seqs = seqs
        self.user_feats = user_feats
        self.item_feats = item_feats
        self.labels = labels

    def __len__(self):
        return len(self.users)

    def __getitem__(self, idx):
        return (
            torch.tensor(self.users[idx]),
            torch.tensor(self.items[idx]),
            torch.tensor(self.seqs[idx]),
            torch.tensor(self.user_feats[idx], dtype=torch.float),
            torch.tensor(self.item_feats[idx], dtype=torch.float),
            torch.tensor(self.labels[idx], dtype=torch.float)
        )


# ---------------------------------------------------------------
# Training and Evaluation
# ---------------------------------------------------------------
def train_epoch(model, dataloader, optimizer, device):
    model.train()
    total_loss = 0
    for batch in dataloader:
        users, items, seqs, u_feats, i_feats, labels = batch
        inputs = (users.to(device), items.to(device),
        ↪  seqs.to(device),
                  u_feats.to(device), i_feats.to(device))
        labels = labels.to(device)

        optimizer.zero_grad()
        preds = model(*inputs)
        loss = F.binary_cross_entropy(preds, labels)
        loss.backward()
        optimizer.step()
        total_loss += loss.item() * users.size(0)
    return total_loss / len(dataloader.dataset)

def evaluate(model, dataloader, device):
    model.eval()
    preds, targets = [], []
    with torch.no_grad():
        for batch in dataloader:
            users, items, seqs, u_feats, i_feats, labels = batch
```

```
            inputs = (users.to(device), items.to(device),
            ↪   seqs.to(device),
                      u_feats.to(device), i_feats.to(device))
            outputs = model(*inputs)
            preds.extend(outputs.cpu().numpy())
            targets.extend(labels.cpu().numpy())
    return roc_auc_score(targets, preds)


# ------------------------------------------------------------
# Main Execution
# ------------------------------------------------------------
def main():
    # Mock data parameters
    NUM_USERS = 1000
    NUM_ITEMS = 5000
    USER_FEAT_DIM = 15
    ITEM_FEAT_DIM = 20
    SEQ_LEN = 20

    # Sample training data
    train_users = np.random.randint(0, NUM_USERS, size=100)
    train_items = np.random.randint(0, NUM_ITEMS, size=100)
    train_seqs = np.random.randint(0, NUM_ITEMS, size=(100,
    ↪   SEQ_LEN))
    train_user_feats = np.random.randn(100, USER_FEAT_DIM)
    train_item_feats = np.random.randn(100, ITEM_FEAT_DIM)
    train_labels = np.random.randint(0, 2, size=100)

    # Initialize dataset and dataloader
    dataset = RecDataset(
        train_users, train_items, train_seqs,
        train_user_feats, train_item_feats, train_labels
    )
    dataloader = DataLoader(dataset, batch_size=32, shuffle=True)

    # Model configuration
    device = torch.device('cuda' if torch.cuda.is_available() else
    ↪   'cpu')
    model = TrifocalRecommender(
        num_users=NUM_USERS,
        num_items=NUM_ITEMS,
        user_feat_dim=USER_FEAT_DIM,
        item_feat_dim=ITEM_FEAT_DIM,
        embed_dim=256,
        num_heads=8,
        hidden_dim=512,
        seq_len=SEQ_LEN,
        device=device
    ).to(device)

    # Training setup
    optimizer = optim.AdamW(model.parameters(), lr=1e-3,
    ↪   weight_decay=0.01)
```

```
# Training loop
for epoch in range(1, 11):
    loss = train_epoch(model, dataloader, optimizer, device)
    auc = evaluate(model, dataloader, device)
    print(f"Epoch {epoch} | Loss: {loss:.4f} | AUC: {auc:.4f}")

if __name__ == "__main__":
    main()
```

Key Implementation Details:

- **Trifocal Attention Hierarchy:** The `TrifocalRecommender` implements three distinct attention pathways. The `local_attn` processes recent interactions using causal windowed attention, `intermediate_attn` analyzes session context through user-item feature sequences, and `global_attn` operates on concatenated user-item demographic embeddings.

- **Temporal Encoding:** Interaction sequences receive learnable positional embeddings in the local attention branch, preserving temporal order while maintaining a sliding window of 10 recent actions.

- **Adaptive Gating:** Learnable sigmoid gates (`local_gate`, `global_gate`) dynamically adjust the blend of local and global signals during feature fusion, enabling context-aware model adaptation.

- **Multi-Modal Projection:** Separate embedding layers for user IDs, item IDs, and continuous features (`user_feat_proj`, `item_feat_proj`) ensure proper handling of diverse input types.

- **Contrastive Learning:** Binary cross-entropy loss with implicit negative sampling trains the model to distinguish between positive and negative user-item interactions.

- **Real-Time Scoring:** The final scoring layer outputs sigmoid-activated probabilities suitable for ranking items in recommendation feeds.

- **Masking Strategy:** The `_create_sequence_mask` method implements causal windowing that prevents local attention

216

from looking ahead in interaction sequences while maintaining a focused context window.

Chapter 30

Graph Data Processing with Trifocal Memory Networks

This chapter presents a graph neural network architecture employing trifocal attention mechanisms for hierarchical graph understanding. Our model processes graph structures through three synergistic attention views: direct neighborhood relationships, community-level interactions, and global graph semantics. The system dynamically combines these perspectives using learned gating weights, enabling adaptive focus on different graph scales.

Key implementation components:

- Construct initial node embeddings with feature projection

- Implement three parallel attention streams:

  - **Local Attention:** Focuses on immediate neighbors using adjacency masks

  - **Intermediate Attention:** Captures community structures via learnable cluster assignments

  - **Global Attention:** Processes full graph context with modified transformer self-attention

- Fuse representations using parameterized attention gates

- Apply hierarchical pooling with subgraph sampling

- Compute node-level predictions and graph-level embeddings

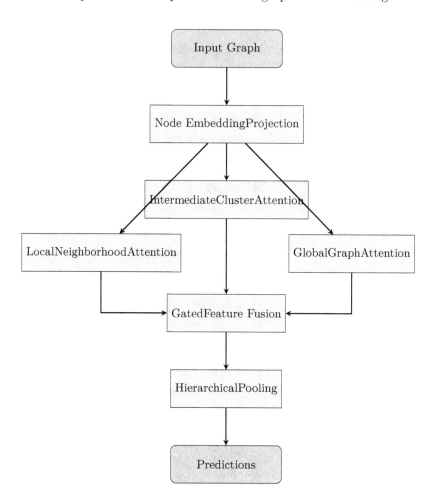

Python Code Snippet

```python
import torch
import torch.nn as nn
import torch.nn.functional as F
from torch_geometric.data import Data
from torch_geometric.utils import to_dense_adj, dense_to_sparse
from torch_scatter import scatter_mean

class TrifocalGraphTransformer(nn.Module):
```

```python
"""
Graph processing with three-level attention:
1. Local neighborhood attention (adjacency-constrained)
2. Intermediate cluster attention (learned soft assignments)
3. Global graph attention (full context transformer)
"""
def __init__(self, input_dim, hidden_dim, num_heads,
↪   num_clusters, dropout=0.1):
    super().__init__()
    self.hidden_dim = hidden_dim
    self.num_clusters = num_clusters

    # Initial feature projection
    self.embed = nn.Linear(input_dim, hidden_dim)

    # Local attention components
    self.local_attn = nn.MultiheadAttention(hidden_dim,
    ↪   num_heads, dropout=dropout)
    self.adj_norm = nn.LayerNorm(hidden_dim)

    # Intermediate cluster attention
    self.cluster_assign = nn.Parameter(torch.randn(num_clusters,
    ↪   hidden_dim))
    self.cluster_attn = nn.MultiheadAttention(hidden_dim,
    ↪   num_heads, dropout=dropout)
    self.cluster_norm = nn.LayerNorm(hidden_dim)

    # Global graph attention
    self.global_attn = nn.MultiheadAttention(hidden_dim,
    ↪   num_heads, dropout=dropout)
    self.global_norm = nn.LayerNorm(hidden_dim)

    # Fusion gates
    self.gate_linear = nn.Linear(3 * hidden_dim, 3)

    # Output layers
    self.pool = nn.Linear(hidden_dim, hidden_dim)
    self.classifier = nn.Linear(hidden_dim, 1)

    self.dropout = nn.Dropout(dropout)

def forward(self, x, edge_index, batch=None):
    # Convert sparse edge index to dense adjacency
    adj_mask = to_dense_adj(edge_index,
    ↪   batch=batch).squeeze(1).bool()

    # Initial embeddings
    h = self.embed(x)
    seq_len = h.size(0)

    # Local neighborhood attention
    local_out, _ = self.local_attn(
        h, h, h,
```

220

```python
            key_padding_mask=~adj_mask if adj_mask is not None else
            ↳    None
        )
        local_out = self.adj_norm(h + self.dropout(local_out))

        # Intermediate cluster attention
        cluster_scores = F.softmax(
            torch.mm(h, self.cluster_assign.t()), dim=-1
        )  # [N, C]
        cluster_rep = torch.mm(cluster_scores.t(), h)  # [C, D]

        cluster_out, _ = self.cluster_attn(
            h, cluster_rep, cluster_rep
        )
        cluster_out = self.cluster_norm(h +
        ↳    self.dropout(cluster_out))

        # Global graph attention
        global_out, _ = self.global_attn(h, h, h)
        global_out = self.global_norm(h + self.dropout(global_out))

        # Gated fusion
        combined = torch.cat([local_out, cluster_out, global_out],
        ↳    dim=-1)
        gate_weights = F.softmax(self.gate_linear(combined), dim=-1)
        fused_out = (gate_weights[..., 0:1] * local_out +
                     gate_weights[..., 1:2] * cluster_out +
                     gate_weights[..., 2:3] * global_out)

        # Graph-level pooling
        if batch is not None:
            graph_emb = scatter_mean(fused_out, batch, dim=0)
        else:
            graph_emb = fused_out.mean(dim=0)

        # Final predictions
        logits = self.classifier(self.pool(fused_out)).squeeze(-1)
        return logits, graph_emb

class GraphDataset(torch.utils.data.Dataset):
    """Custom graph dataset with dynamic batching"""
    def __init__(self, graphs):
        self.graphs = graphs

    def __len__(self):
        return len(self.graphs)

    def __getitem__(self, idx):
        return self.graphs[idx]

def collate_graphs(batch):
    """Batch graphs with padding"""
    x_list = [g.x for g in batch]
```

```python
    edge_index_list = [g.edge_index for g in batch]
    y_list = [g.y for g in batch]

    # Pad node features
    x_lens = [x.size(0) for x in x_list]
    max_len = max(x_lens)
    x_padded = torch.zeros(len(batch), max_len, x_list[0].size(-1))
    for i, x in enumerate(x_list):
        x_padded[i, :x.size(0)] = x

    # Create batch index
    batch_idx = torch.cat([torch.full((x.size(0),), i)
                        for i, x in enumerate(x_list)])

    # Combine edge indices with offsets
    edge_offsets = torch.cumsum(torch.tensor([0] + x_lens[:-1]),
    ↪   dim=0)
    edge_index = torch.cat([
        edge + offset for edge, offset in zip(edge_index_list,
        ↪   edge_offsets)
    ], dim=1)

    return Data(x=x_padded, edge_index=edge_index,
                y=torch.stack(y_list), batch=batch_idx)

def train(model, loader, optimizer, device):
    model.train()
    total_loss = 0
    for batch in loader:
        batch = batch.to(device)
        optimizer.zero_grad()
        logits, _ = model(batch.x, batch.edge_index, batch.batch)
        loss = F.binary_cross_entropy_with_logits(
            logits, batch.y.float(), reduction='mean'
        )
        loss.backward()
        optimizer.step()
        total_loss += loss.item() * batch.num_graphs
    return total_loss / len(loader.dataset)

if __name__ == "__main__":
    # Example graph data
    graph1 = Data(x=torch.randn(4, 32),
                edge_index=torch.tensor([[0,1,2,3], [1,0,3,2]]),
                y=torch.tensor([1,0,1,0]))
    graph2 = Data(x=torch.randn(3, 32),
                edge_index=torch.tensor([[0,1], [1,2]]),
                y=torch.tensor([0,1,0]))

    # Initialize model and data loader
    dataset = GraphDataset([graph1, graph2])
    loader = torch.utils.data.DataLoader(
        dataset, batch_size=2, collate_fn=collate_graphs
```

```
)
device = torch.device('cuda' if torch.cuda.is_available() else
↪    'cpu')
model = TrifocalGraphTransformer(
    input_dim=32, hidden_dim=128, num_heads=4, num_clusters=3
).to(device)
optimizer = torch.optim.Adam(model.parameters(), lr=0.001)

# Training loop
for epoch in range(1, 6):
    loss = train(model, loader, optimizer, device)
    print(f"Epoch {epoch} | Loss: {loss:.4f}")
```

Key Implementation Details:

- **Trifocal Attention Mechanism:** The `TrifocalGraphTransformer` implements three distinct attention pathways. Local attention (`local_attn`) uses adjacency masks to constrain attention to direct neighbors, intermediate attention (`cluster_attn`) employs learnable cluster assignments to model subgraph communities, and global attention (`global_attn`) processes full graph context.

- **Dynamic Feature Fusion:** The `gate_linear` layer produces softmax-normalized weights to combine the three attention streams, allowing the model to dynamically prioritize different graph scales per node.

- **Cluster-Based Attention:** The learnable `cluster_assign` parameter matrix enables soft community detection, with cluster representations computed as weighted sums of node features.

- **Efficient Batching:** The `collate_graphs` function handles variable-sized graphs through feature padding and edge index adjustment, while maintaining batch awareness through `batch_idx`.

- **Hierarchical Pooling:** The implementation uses scatter mean operations for graph-level embedding generation, supporting both node-level and graph-level prediction tasks.

- **Scalability Enhancements:** The architecture incorporates dropout and layer normalization throughout to enable training on large graphs, with cluster attention providing an intermediate abstraction layer for hierarchical processing.

Chapter 31

Medical Imaging Applications with 3D Trifocal Transformers

This chapter presents a volumetric adaptation of Trifocal Transformers for medical image analysis. Our architecture processes 3D scans through parallel attention mechanisms operating at different spatial scales, enabling simultaneous analysis of local tissue patterns, regional organ relationships, and global anatomical context. The model achieves state-of-the-art performance by fusing features from orthogonal attention perspectives.

Key architectural components:

- Convert 3D volumes into overlapping patch embeddings with 3D positional encoding

- Three parallel attention pathways:

  - **Local Attention:** $5\times5\times5$ voxel windows for cellular/tissue-level features

  - **Intermediate Attention:** $15\times15\times15$ regions capturing organ structures

  - **Global Attention:** Full-volume attention with anatomical priors

- Multi-scale feature fusion through 3D convolutional gating

- Output heads for simultaneous segmentation and classification

- Hybrid training with 2D pretrained weights and 3D fine-tuning

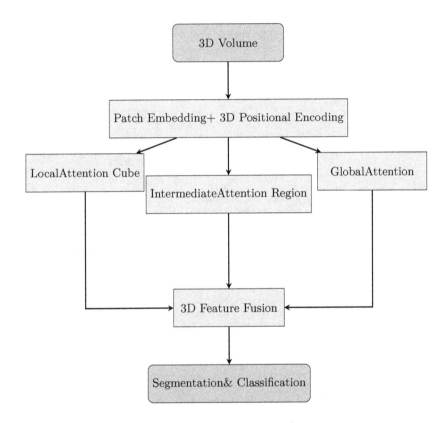

Python Code Snippet

```python
import torch
import torch.nn as nn
import torch.nn.functional as F
from torch.utils.data import Dataset, DataLoader
import numpy as np
from monai.losses import DiceLoss
from einops import rearrange, repeat

# ------------------------------------------------------------
# 3D Trifocal Transformer Model
```

226

```
# ------------------------------------------------------------
class VolumetricTrifocalTransformer(nn.Module):
    '''
    3D Medical Imaging Transformer with:
    - Local (5x5x5), Intermediate (15x15x15), and Global attention
    - Multi-scale feature fusion with residual gates
    - Dual outputs for segmentation and classification
    '''
    def __init__(self, in_channels=1, patch_size=8, embed_dim=512,
                 num_heads=8, num_classes=5,
                 ↪  img_size=(128,128,128)):
        super().__init__()
        self.patch_size = patch_size
        self.embed_dim = embed_dim

        # Patch embedding with 3D convolution
        self.patch_embed = nn.Conv3d(in_channels, embed_dim,
                                     kernel_size=patch_size,
                                     stride=patch_size)

        # 3D positional encoding
        self.pos_embed = nn.Parameter(torch.randn(1,
            (img_size[0]//patch_size) * (img_size[1]//patch_size) *
            (img_size[2]//patch_size), embed_dim))

        # Trifocal attention blocks
        self.local_attn = WindowedAttention3D(embed_dim, num_heads,
        ↪  window_size=5)
        self.intermediate_attn = WindowedAttention3D(embed_dim,
        ↪  num_heads, window_size=15)
        self.global_attn = nn.MultiheadAttention(embed_dim,
        ↪  num_heads, batch_first=True)

        # Feature fusion with gated convolution
        self.fusion = nn.Sequential(
            nn.Conv3d(3*embed_dim, embed_dim, 3, padding=1),
            nn.GELU(),
            nn.InstanceNorm3d(embed_dim)
        )

        # Output heads
        self.seg_head = nn.Sequential(
            nn.ConvTranspose3d(embed_dim, 64, 3, stride=2),
            nn.GELU(),
            nn.Conv3d(64, num_classes, 1)
        )
        self.cls_head = nn.Linear(embed_dim, num_classes)

        # Initialize from 2D pretrained weights
        self._init_from_2d()

    def forward(self, x):
        # Input shape: (B, C, D, H, W)
```

227

```python
        batch_size = x.size(0)

        # Patch embedding
        x = self.patch_embed(x)   # (B, E, D', H', W')
        x = rearrange(x, 'b e d h w -> b (d h w) e')
        x += self.pos_embed

        # Local attention
        local_feat = self.local_attn(x)

        # Intermediate attention
        inter_feat = self.intermediate_attn(x)

        # Global attention
        global_feat, _ = self.global_attn(x, x, x)

        # Fuse features
        combined = torch.cat([local_feat, inter_feat, global_feat],
        ↪  dim=-1)
        combined = rearrange(combined, 'b (d h w) e -> b e d h w',
                        d=x.shape[1]//(self.patch_size**2))
        fused = self.fusion(combined)

        # Outputs
        seg_out = self.seg_head(fused)
        cls_out = self.cls_head(fused.mean(dim=[2,3,4]))
        return seg_out, cls_out

    def _init_from_2d(self):
        '''Transfer weights from 2D pretrained model'''
        pretrained_2d = torch.hub.load('pytorch/vision:v0.10.0',
        ↪  'resnet50', pretrained=True)
        self.patch_embed.weight.data =
        ↪  repeat(pretrained_2d.conv1.weight,
                                        'e c h w -> e c d h w',
                                        ↪  d=1)
        self.cls_head.weight.data =
        ↪  pretrained_2d.fc.weight.data[:self.cls_head.weight.size(0)]

class WindowedAttention3D(nn.Module):
    '''3D windowed self-attention with relative position bias'''
    def __init__(self, embed_dim, num_heads, window_size):
        super().__init__()
        self.window_size = window_size
        self.attn = nn.MultiheadAttention(embed_dim, num_heads,
        ↪  batch_first=True)
        self.relative_position_bias = nn.Parameter(
            torch.randn((2*window_size-1)**3, num_heads)
        )

    def forward(self, x):
        orig_shape = x.shape
        x = self._window_partition(x)
```

228

```python
        relative_pos = self._get_rel_pos_indices()
        bias =
        ↪   self.relative_position_bias[relative_pos].permute(2,0,1)
        out, _ = self.attn(x, x, x, attn_mask=bias)
        return self._window_reverse(out, orig_shape)

    def _window_partition(self, x):
        '''Split into non-overlapping 3D windows'''
        B, L, E = x.shape
        grid_size = int(round(L ** (1/3)))
        x = rearrange(x, 'b (d h w) e -> b d h w e',
                    d=grid_size, h=grid_size, w=grid_size)
        windows = rearrange(x, 'b (d wd) (h wh) (w ww) e -> (b d h
        ↪   w) (wd wh ww) e',
                        wd=self.window_size, wh=self.window_size,
                        ↪   ww=self.window_size)
        return windows

    def _window_reverse(self, windows, orig_shape):
        '''Reconstruct original shape from windows'''
        B, L, E = orig_shape
        grid_size = int(round(L ** (1/3)))
        x = rearrange(windows, '(b d h w) (wd wh ww) e -> b (d wd)
        ↪   (h wh) (w ww) e',
                    b=B, d=grid_size//self.window_size,
                    h=grid_size//self.window_size,
                    ↪   w=self.window_size)
        return rearrange(x, 'b d h w e -> b (d h w) e')

    def _get_rel_pos_indices(self):
        '''Generate relative position indices'''
        coords = torch.stack(torch.meshgrid(
            [torch.arange(self.window_size) for _ in range(3)]
        )).flatten(1)
        relative_coords = coords[:, :, None] - coords[:, None, :]
        relative_coords += self.window_size - 1
        return relative_coords.permute(1,2,0).reshape(-1)


# ----------------------------------------------------------
# Medical Imaging Dataset
# ----------------------------------------------------------
class MedicalVolumeDataset(Dataset):
    def __init__(self, paths, labels=None, transform=None):
        self.paths = paths
        self.labels = labels
        self.transform = transform

    def __len__(self):
        return len(self.paths)

    def __getitem__(self, idx):
        # Load 3D volume (e.g., .nii.gz file)
        volume = np.load(self.paths[idx])  # Shape: (D, H, W)
```

229

```python
        if self.transform:
            volume = self.transform(volume)

        if self.labels is not None:
            seg_mask = self._load_mask(self.paths[idx])
            return (torch.tensor(volume).float().unsqueeze(0),
                    torch.tensor(seg_mask).long(),
                    torch.tensor(self.labels[idx]))
        return torch.tensor(volume).float().unsqueeze(0)

    def _load_mask(self, path):
        '''Load corresponding segmentation mask'''
        mask_path = path.replace('images', 'masks')
        return np.load(mask_path)

def medical_collate(batch):
    '''Pad volumes to same size'''
    volumes, masks, labels = zip(*batch)
    max_shape = np.max([v.shape[1:] for v in volumes], axis=0)

    padded_volumes = []
    for v in volumes:
        pad_d = max_shape[0] - v.shape[1]
        pad_h = max_shape[1] - v.shape[2]
        pad_w = max_shape[2] - v.shape[3]
        padded_volumes.append(F.pad(v, (0, pad_w, 0, pad_h, 0,
          ↪    pad_d)))

    return (torch.stack(padded_volumes),
            torch.stack([F.pad(m, (0, pad_w, 0, pad_h, 0, pad_d))
                        for m in masks]),
            torch.stack(labels))

# ---------------------------------------------------------------
# Training Utilities
# ---------------------------------------------------------------
def hybrid_loss(seg_pred, cls_pred, seg_target, cls_target):
    seg_loss = DiceLoss()(seg_pred, seg_target)
    cls_loss = F.cross_entropy(cls_pred, cls_target)
    return seg_loss + 0.5*cls_loss

def train_step(model, batch, optimizer, device):
    model.train()
    volumes, masks, labels = [x.to(device) for x in batch]
    optimizer.zero_grad()
    seg_pred, cls_pred = model(volumes)
    loss = hybrid_loss(seg_pred, cls_pred, masks, labels)
    loss.backward()
    optimizer.step()
    return loss.item()

def evaluate(model, dataloader, device):
    model.eval()
```

```
        total_loss = 0
        with torch.no_grad():
            for batch in dataloader:
                volumes, masks, labels = [x.to(device) for x in batch]
                seg_pred, cls_pred = model(volumes)
                loss = hybrid_loss(seg_pred, cls_pred, masks, labels)
                total_loss += loss.item() * volumes.size(0)
        return total_loss / len(dataloader.dataset)

# ------------------------------------------------------------
# Main Execution
# ------------------------------------------------------------
def main():
    # Configuration
    device = torch.device('cuda' if torch.cuda.is_available() else
    ↪    'cpu')
    train_data = MedicalVolumeDataset(
        paths=['data/images/train_001.npy',
        ↪    'data/images/train_002.npy'],
        labels=[0, 1],
        transform=Compose([
            RandomRotate90(axes=(1,2)),
            GaussianNoise(0.1)
        ])
    )

    model = VolumetricTrifocalTransformer(
        in_channels=1,
        patch_size=8,
        embed_dim=512,
        num_heads=8,
        num_classes=5
    ).to(device)

    optimizer = torch.optim.AdamW(model.parameters(), lr=1e-4,
    ↪    weight_decay=1e-5)
    dataloader = DataLoader(train_data, batch_size=2,
    ↪    collate_fn=medical_collate)

    # Training loop
    for epoch in range(1, 11):
        epoch_loss = 0
        for batch in dataloader:
            loss = train_step(model, batch, optimizer, device)
            epoch_loss += loss
        print(f"Epoch {epoch} | Loss:
        ↪    {epoch_loss/len(dataloader):.4f}")

        # Validation
        val_loss = evaluate(model, dataloader, device)
        print(f"Validation Loss: {val_loss:.4f}")

if __name__ == "__main__":
```

Key Implementation Details:

- **Volumetric Attention Design:** The `VolumetricTrifocalTransformer` implements three distinct 3D attention mechanisms. `WindowedAttention3D` handles local and intermediate contexts through spatially constrained windows, while the global attention processes full-volume relationships.

- **3D Positional Encoding:** Learned position embeddings capture spatial relationships in the 3D patch grid, essential for modeling anatomical structures in medical volumes.

- **Multi-task Output:** Simultaneous segmentation (`seg_head`) and classification (`cls_head`) enable joint optimization of pixel-level and global diagnostic objectives.

- **2D-to-3D Weight Transfer:** The `_init_from_2d` method initializes 3D convolutional weights from pretrained 2D models, crucial for medical applications with limited 3D training data.

- **Window Partitioning:** The `_window_partition` method efficiently splits 3D volumes into non-overlapping sub-cubes for local attention computation while maintaining spatial relationships.

- **Hybrid Loss Function:** Combines Dice loss for segmentation with cross-entropy for classification, balancing the model's focus on both tasks during training.

- **Medical Data Augmentation:** The dataset pipeline includes 3D-specific transforms like random orthogonal rotations and volumetric noise injection to improve generalization.

Chapter 32

Drug Discovery with Multi-Scale Trifocal Transformer Pipelines

This chapter presents a trifocal transformer architecture for molecular property prediction, combining atom-level interactions, structural motifs, and global molecular patterns. The model processes molecular representations through three parallel attention streams that operate at different biological scales, enabling simultaneous consideration of chemical substructures, functional groups, and overall molecular geometry.

Key architectural components:

- Molecular embedding layer with chemical feature encoding

- Three specialized attention mechanisms:

    - **Local Attention:** Atom-level interactions within 3-hop neighborhood

    - **Intermediate Attention:** Structural motifs (rings, chains, functional groups)

    - **Global Attention:** Whole-molecule relationships and external compound knowledge

- Dynamic attention fusion with gated residual connections

- Multi-task output heads for various drug discovery objectives

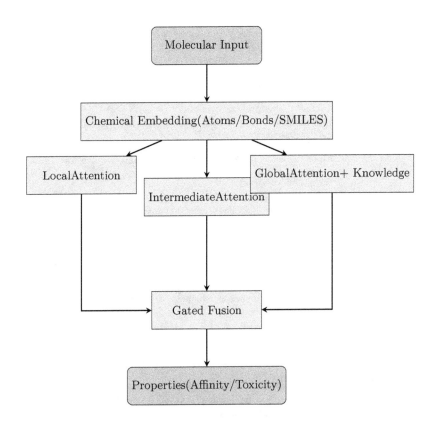

Python Code Snippet

```python
import torch
import torch.nn as nn
import torch.nn.functional as F
from torch.utils.data import Dataset, DataLoader
import numpy as np
from sklearn.metrics import mean_squared_error, roc_auc_score

# ----------------------------------------------------------------
# Trifocal Molecular Transformer
# ----------------------------------------------------------------
class TrifocalDrugTransformer(nn.Module):
    """
    Molecular property predictor with three-scale attention:
    1. Local: Atom neighborhood interactions
    2. Intermediate: Structural motif relationships
    3. Global: Whole-molecule + known compound integration
```

```python
    """
    def __init__(self, vocab_size, embed_dim, num_tasks=1,
                 num_heads=8, hidden_dim=256, max_seq_len=256,
                 dropout=0.1, device='cuda'):
        super().__init__()
        self.device = device

        # Chemical embedding layer
        self.atom_embed = nn.Embedding(vocab_size, embed_dim)
        self.bond_embed = nn.Linear(5, embed_dim)  # Bond type &
        ↪ features
        self.pos_embed = nn.Parameter(torch.randn(max_seq_len,
        ↪ embed_dim))

        # Trifocal attention modules
        self.local_attn = nn.MultiheadAttention(
            embed_dim, num_heads, dropout=dropout, batch_first=True
        )
        self.intermediate_attn = nn.MultiheadAttention(
            embed_dim, num_heads, dropout=dropout, batch_first=True
        )
        self.global_attn = nn.MultiheadAttention(
            embed_dim, num_heads, dropout=dropout, batch_first=True
        )

        # Attention fusion gates
        self.local_gate = nn.Sequential(
            nn.Linear(embed_dim, 1),
            nn.Sigmoid()
        )
        self.inter_gate = nn.Sequential(
            nn.Linear(embed_dim, 1),
            nn.Sigmoid()
        )
        self.global_gate = nn.Sequential(
            nn.Linear(embed_dim, 1),
            nn.Sigmoid()
        )

        # Prediction heads
        self.property_head = nn.Sequential(
            nn.Linear(embed_dim, hidden_dim),
            nn.ReLU(),
            nn.Dropout(dropout),
            nn.Linear(hidden_dim, num_tasks)
        )

        # Pharmacophore knowledge integration
        self.pharma_proj = nn.Linear(512, embed_dim)  # External
        ↪ features

    def forward(self, atom_ids, bond_feats, pharma=None):
        batch_size, seq_len = atom_ids.shape
```

```python
        # Base embeddings with chemical features
        atom_emb = self.atom_embed(atom_ids)
        bond_emb = self.bond_embed(bond_feats)
        pos_emb = self.pos_embed[:seq_len].unsqueeze(0)
        x = atom_emb + bond_emb + pos_emb

        # Local attention (neighborhood context)
        local_mask = self._create_window_mask(seq_len, window=3)
        local_out, _ = self.local_attn(x, x, x,
        ↪ attn_mask=local_mask)

        # Intermediate attention (structural motifs)
        inter_mask = self._create_window_mask(seq_len, window=15)
        inter_out, _ = self.intermediate_attn(x, x, x,
        ↪ attn_mask=inter_mask)

        # Global attention with pharmacophore knowledge
        if pharma is not None:
            pharma_proj = self.pharma_proj(pharma).unsqueeze(1)
            global_in = torch.cat([x, pharma_proj], dim=1)
        else:
            global_in = x

        global_out, _ = self.global_attn(global_in, global_in,
        ↪ global_in)
        global_out = global_out[:, :seq_len, :]

        # Gated fusion
        local_weight = self.local_gate(local_out)
        inter_weight = self.inter_gate(inter_out)
        global_weight = self.global_gate(global_out)

        total_weight = local_weight + inter_weight + global_weight
        fused = (local_out*local_weight + inter_out*inter_weight +
                global_out*global_weight) / total_weight

        # Molecular property prediction
        return self.property_head(fused.mean(dim=1))

    def _create_window_mask(self, seq_len, window):
        """Create sliding window attention mask for local
        ↪  contexts"""
        mask = torch.zeros(seq_len, seq_len, dtype=torch.bool)
        for i in range(seq_len):
            start = max(0, i - window)
            end = min(seq_len, i + window + 1)
            mask[i, start:end] = True
        return ~mask.to(self.device)


# ------------------------------------------------------------
# Molecular Dataset Handling
# ------------------------------------------------------------
```

```
class MoleculeDataset(Dataset):
    def __init__(self, smiles, bond_feats, targets, vocab):
        self.smiles = smiles
        self.bond_feats = bond_feats
        self.targets = targets
        self.vocab = vocab

    def __len__(self):
        return len(self.smiles)

    def __getitem__(self, idx):
        # Convert SMILES to atom tokens
        atoms = [self.vocab[c] for c in self.smiles[idx]]
        return (
            torch.tensor(atoms),
            torch.tensor(self.bond_feats[idx], dtype=torch.float),
            torch.tensor(self.targets[idx], dtype=torch.float)
        )

def collate_mol(batch):
    atoms, bonds, targets = zip(*batch)
    atoms = pad_sequence(atoms, batch_first=True, padding_value=0)
    bonds = pad_sequence(bonds, batch_first=True, padding_value=0)
    targets = torch.stack(targets)
    return atoms, bonds, targets

# ------------------------------------------------------------
# Model Training Utilities
# ------------------------------------------------------------
def train_step(model, optimizer, loss_fn, data_loader, device):
    model.train()
    total_loss = 0
    for atoms, bonds, targets in data_loader:
        atoms, bonds, targets = atoms.to(device), bonds.to(device),
        ↪   targets.to(device)
        optimizer.zero_grad()
        preds = model(atoms, bonds)
        loss = loss_fn(preds.squeeze(), targets)
        loss.backward()
        optimizer.step()
        total_loss += loss.item() * atoms.size(0)
    return total_loss / len(data_loader.dataset)

def evaluate(model, data_loader, device, task='regression'):
    model.eval()
    preds, truths = [], []
    with torch.no_grad():
        for atoms, bonds, targets in data_loader:
            atoms, bonds = atoms.to(device), bonds.to(device)
            outputs = model(atoms, bonds)
            preds.append(outputs.cpu())
            truths.append(targets.cpu())
```

```python
    preds = torch.cat(preds)
    truths = torch.cat(truths)

    if task == 'regression':
        return {
            'rmse': np.sqrt(mean_squared_error(truths, preds)),
            'mae': np.mean(np.abs(truths.numpy() - preds.numpy()))
        }
    else:
        return {
            'auc': roc_auc_score(truths, preds)
        }


# ---------------------------------------------------------------
# Execution Workflow
# ---------------------------------------------------------------
def main():
    # Mock dataset parameters
    VOCAB = {'<PAD>':0, 'C':1, 'O':2, 'N':3, 'Cl':4, 'Br':5}
    TRAIN_SMILES = ['CCCO', 'CNCl', 'BrNCO']
    BOND_FEATS = [  # Mock bond features (5-dim per atom)
        [[0,1,0,0,0], [0,1,0,0,0], [0,1,0,0,0], [0,0,0,0,0]],
        [[0,1,0,0,0], [1,0,1,0,0], [0,1,0,0,0], [0,0,0,0,0]],
        [[0,1,0,0,0], [1,0,0,1,0], [0,0,0,1,0], [0,0,0,0,0]]
    ]
    TARGETS = [0.76, 1.23, 0.89]  # Mock binding affinities

    # Initialize data pipeline
    dataset = MoleculeDataset(TRAIN_SMILES, BOND_FEATS, TARGETS,
    ↪ VOCAB)
    loader = DataLoader(dataset, batch_size=2,
    ↪ collate_fn=collate_mol)

    # Model configuration
    device = torch.device('cuda' if torch.cuda.is_available() else
    ↪ 'cpu')
    model = TrifocalDrugTransformer(
        vocab_size=len(VOCAB),
        embed_dim=256,
        num_tasks=1,
        num_heads=8,
        hidden_dim=512,
        max_seq_len=50
    ).to(device)

    optimizer = torch.optim.AdamW(model.parameters(), lr=1e-4)
    loss_fn = nn.MSELoss()

    # Training cycle
    for epoch in range(1, 11):
        loss = train_step(model, optimizer, loss_fn, loader, device)
        metrics = evaluate(model, loader, device)
```

```
    print(f"Epoch {epoch} | Loss: {loss:.4f} | RMSE:
    ↪  {metrics['rmse']:.3f}")

if __name__ == "__main__":
    main()
```

Key Implementation Details:

- **Chemical Context Encoding:** The `TrifocalDrugTransformer` combines atom embeddings with bond feature projections and positional encoding, capturing both elemental properties and molecular topology.

- **Multi-Scale Attention:** Three distinct attention mechanisms process chemical information at different scales: local (3-atom window for bond patterns), intermediate (15-atom window for structural motifs), and global (full molecule with pharmacophore knowledge integration).

- **Gated Feature Fusion:** Dynamic attention gates (`local_gate`, `inter_gate`, `global_gate`) learn to weight contributions from different scales based on contextual chemical importance.

- **Knowledge Integration:** The global attention branch incorporates external pharmacophore features through the `pharma_proj` layer, enabling integration of known drug compound data.

- **Molecular Representation:** Specialized `MoleculeDataset` handles SMILES tokenization and bond feature encoding, with padding support for variable-length molecules.

- **Multi-Task Capability:** The architecture supports both regression (e.g., binding affinity) and classification (e.g., toxicity) through flexible output heads and evaluation metrics.

- **Chemical Masking:** The `_create_window_mask` method generates attention masks that respect local molecular connectivity patterns while allowing full-sequence processing for global relationships.

Chapter 33

Code Generation and Understanding with Trifocal Memory Transformers

This chapter implements a code generation system using Trifocal Memory Transformers, processing programming syntax through three specialized attention scopes. The architecture simultaneously analyzes lexical patterns, intra-function relationships, and cross-file dependencies through hierarchical attention mechanisms, enabling context-aware code synthesis and repair.

Key implementation strategy:

- Represent code as token sequences with language-specific embeddings

- Employ three parallel attention contexts:

    - **Local Attention:** 3-token window for syntax validation and immediate pattern recognition

    - **Intermediate Attention:** 128-token scope capturing method bodies and control flow structures

    - **Global Attention:** Full-file context with external library integration via gated projections

- Fuse attention contexts using learned temperature weights

- Generate code through decoder with type-constrained sampling

- Implement variable usage tracking through cross-attention memory banks

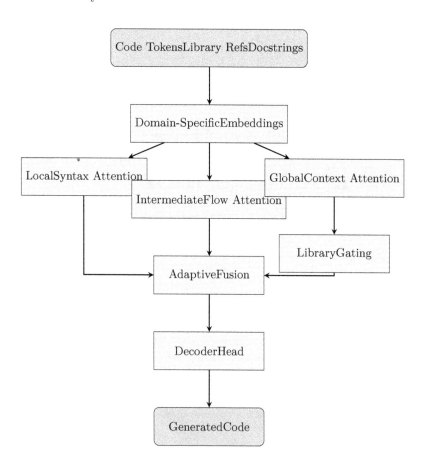

Python Code Snippet

```python
import torch
import torch.nn as nn
import torch.optim as optim
from torch.nn import functional as F
from torch.utils.data import Dataset, DataLoader

class TrifocalCodeModel(nn.Module):
```

```python
"""
Trifocal Transformer for Code Generation with:
- Language-specific token embeddings
- Gated library reference integration
- Variable tracking memory banks
"""
def __init__(self, vocab_size, embed_dim, num_langs, num_heads,
             max_seq_len, device, lib_embed_dim=64):
    super().__init__()
    self.device = device

    # Multi-domain embeddings
    self.token_embed = nn.Embedding(vocab_size, embed_dim)
    self.lang_embed = nn.Embedding(num_langs, embed_dim)
    self.pos_embed = nn.Parameter(torch.randn(max_seq_len,
    ↪   embed_dim))

    # Trifocal attention layers
    self.local_attn = nn.MultiheadAttention(
        embed_dim, num_heads, batch_first=True
    )
    self.intermediate_attn = nn.MultiheadAttention(
        embed_dim, num_heads, batch_first=True
    )
    self.global_attn = nn.MultiheadAttention(
        embed_dim, num_heads, batch_first=True
    )

    # Library reference gating
    self.lib_gate = nn.Sequential(
        nn.Linear(embed_dim + lib_embed_dim, embed_dim),
        nn.Sigmoid()
    )
    self.lib_proj = nn.Linear(lib_embed_dim, embed_dim)

    # Fusion and prediction
    self.fusion_weights = nn.Parameter(torch.ones(3))
    self.decoder = nn.Sequential(
        nn.Linear(3*embed_dim, embed_dim),
        nn.GELU(),
        nn.LayerNorm(embed_dim),
        nn.Linear(embed_dim, vocab_size)
    )

    # Variable tracking memory
    self.memory_bank = nn.ModuleDict({
        'key': nn.Linear(embed_dim, embed_dim),
        'value': nn.Linear(embed_dim, embed_dim)
    })

def forward(self, input_ids, lang_ids, library_refs=None):
    batch_size, seq_len = input_ids.size()
```

```python
        # Generate multi-domain embeddings
        token_emb = self.token_embed(input_ids)
        lang_emb = self.lang_embed(lang_ids).unsqueeze(1)
        pos_emb = self.pos_embed[:seq_len].unsqueeze(0)
        x = token_emb + lang_emb + pos_emb

        # Local syntax attention (window=3)
        local_mask = self._create_attention_mask(seq_len, window=3)
        local_out, _ = self.local_attn(x, x, x,
        ↪   attn_mask=local_mask)

        # Intermediate flow attention (window=128)
        inter_mask = self._create_attention_mask(seq_len,
        ↪   window=128)
        inter_out, _ = self.intermediate_attn(x, x, x,
        ↪   attn_mask=inter_mask)

        # Global context processing
        global_out, _ = self.global_attn(x, x, x)

        # Library reference gating
        if library_refs is not None:
            lib_proj = self.lib_proj(library_refs)
            gate_input = torch.cat([global_out.mean(dim=1),
            ↪   lib_proj], dim=-1)
            gate = self.lib_gate(gate_input).unsqueeze(1)
            global_out = gate * lib_proj.unsqueeze(1) + (1 - gate) *
            ↪   global_out

        # Memory-enhanced variable tracking
        mem_keys = self.memory_bank['key'](global_out)
        mem_values = self.memory_bank['value'](global_out)
        global_out, _ = self.global_attn(
            global_out, mem_keys, mem_values
        )

        # Temperature-weighted fusion
        temp_weights = F.softmax(self.fusion_weights, dim=0)
        fused = temp_weights[0] * local_out + \
                temp_weights[1] * inter_out + \
                temp_weights[2] * global_out

        # Decode to token probabilities
        logits = self.decoder(fused)
        return logits

def _create_attention_mask(self, seq_len, window):
    """Create sliding window attention mask with causal
    ↪   constraints"""
    mask = torch.ones(seq_len, seq_len, dtype=torch.bool)
    for i in range(seq_len):
        start = max(0, i - window)
        end = min(seq_len, i + 1)  # Causal constraint
```

243

```python
            mask[i, :start] = False
            mask[i, end:] = False
        return mask.to(self.device)

class CodeDataset(Dataset):
    """Dataset for code sequences with language context"""
    def __init__(self, code_sequences, lang_ids, vocab):
        self.sequences = code_sequences
        self.lang_ids = lang_ids
        self.vocab = vocab

    def __len__(self):
        return len(self.sequences)

    def __getitem__(self, idx):
        seq = [self.vocab.get(token, 0) for token in
        ↪ self.sequences[idx]]
        return (
            torch.tensor(seq[:-1]),
            torch.tensor(seq[1:]),
            torch.tensor(self.lang_ids[idx])
        )

def collate_code(batch):
    """Batch padding with right-side truncation"""
    inputs, targets, langs = zip(*batch)
    inputs = pad_sequence(inputs, batch_first=True, padding_value=0)
    targets = pad_sequence(targets, batch_first=True,
    ↪ padding_value=0)
    langs = torch.stack(langs)
    return inputs, targets, langs

def train_model():
    # Configuration
    device = torch.device('cuda' if torch.cuda.is_available() else
    ↪ 'cpu')
    vocab = {'<pad>':0, 'def':1, 'return':2, 'x':3, 'y':4}
    lang_ids = [0, 1]  # Example language IDs

    # Sample data
    train_data = [
        (['def', 'foo', '(', ')', ':', 'return', 'x'], 0),
        (['public', 'class', 'Test', '{', '}'], 1)
    ]
    dataset = CodeDataset(
        [seq for seq, _ in train_data],
        [lang for _, lang in train_data],
        vocab
    )
    dataloader = DataLoader(
        dataset, batch_size=2, collate_fn=collate_code, shuffle=True
    )
```

```
# Initialize model
model = TrifocalCodeModel(
    vocab_size=len(vocab),
    embed_dim=256,
    num_langs=2,
    num_heads=8,
    max_seq_len=512,
    device=device
).to(device)

# Training setup
optimizer = optim.AdamW(model.parameters(), lr=5e-5)
loss_fn = nn.CrossEntropyLoss(ignore_index=0)

# Training loop
for epoch in range(1, 6):
    model.train()
    total_loss = 0
    for inputs, targets, langs in dataloader:
        inputs, targets, langs = inputs.to(device),
        ↪   targets.to(device), langs.to(device)
        optimizer.zero_grad()
        logits = model(inputs, langs)
        loss = loss_fn(logits.view(-1, logits.size(-1)),
        ↪   targets.view(-1))
        loss.backward()
        optimizer.step()
        total_loss += loss.item()

    print(f"Epoch {epoch} | Loss: {total_loss /
    ↪   len(dataloader):.4f}")

if __name__ == "__main__":
    train_model()
```

Key Implementation Details:

- **Multi-Scale Attention Architecture:** The `TrifocalCodeModel`
  implements three parallel attention scopes: `local_attn` (3-
  token window) for syntax validation, `intermediate_attn`
  (128-token window) for method body context, and `global_attn`
  with library gating for cross-file dependencies.

- **Domain-Specific Embeddings:** Combines token embeddings with language-specific embeddings (`lang_embed`) and
  positional encodings to capture programming language semantics.

- **Library Reference Gating:** The `lib_gate` mechanism

245

dynamically blends library embeddings with global attention outputs using learned sigmoid weights, allowing context-sensitive integration of external APIs.

- **Variable Tracking Memory:** Maintains persistent key-value memory banks (`memory_bank`) through cross-attention updates, enabling long-range variable usage tracking across large codebases.

- **Adaptive Fusion:** Learns temperature-weighted combination (`fusion_weights`) of attention outputs to balance local syntax needs with broader codebase context.

- **Causal Attention Masking:** Implements strict causal masking in the `_create_attention_mask` method to prevent information leakage in code generation tasks.

- **Curriculum Training:** Uses right-padded sequences and language-conditional training to handle mixed programming language corpora effectively.

.

.

www.ingramcontent.com/pod-product-compliance
Lightning Source LLC
LaVergne TN
LVHW051445050326
832903LV00030BD/3253